C-137   CAREER EXAMINATION SERIES

This is your
PASSBOOK for...

Civil Engineering Draftsman

Test Preparation Study Guide
Questions & Answers

COPYRIGHT NOTICE

This book is SOLELY intended for, is sold ONLY to, and its use is RESTRICTED to individual, bona fide applicants or candidates who qualify by virtue of having seriously filed applications for appropriate license, certificate, professional and/or promotional advancement, higher school matriculation, scholarship, or other legitimate requirements of education and/or governmental authorities.

This book is NOT intended for use, class instruction, tutoring, training, duplication, copying, reprinting, excerption, or adaptation, etc., by:

1) Other publishers
2) Proprietors and/or Instructors of "Coaching" and/or Preparatory Courses
3) Personnel and/or Training Divisions of commercial, industrial, and governmental organizations
4) Schools, colleges, or universities and/or their departments and staffs, including teachers and other personnel
5) Testing Agencies or Bureaus
6) Study groups which seek by the purchase of a single volume to copy and/or duplicate and/or adapt this material for use by the group as a whole without having purchased individual volumes for each of the members of the group
7) Et al.

Such persons would be in violation of appropriate Federal and State statutes.

PROVISION OF LICENSING AGREEMENTS – Recognized educational, commercial, industrial, and governmental institutions and organizations, and others legitimately engaged in educational pursuits, including training, testing, and measurement activities, may address request for a licensing agreement to the copyright owners, who will determine whether, and under what conditions, including fees and charges, the materials in this book may be used them. In other words, a licensing facility exists for the legitimate use of the material in this book on other than an individual basis. However, it is asseverated and affirmed here that the material in this book CANNOT be used without the receipt of the express permission of such a licensing agreement from the Publishers. Inquiries re licensing should be addressed to the company, attention rights and permissions department.

All rights reserved, including the right of reproduction in whole or in part, in any form or by any means, electronic or mechanical, including photocopying, recording, or by any information storage and retrieval system, without permission in writing from the Publisher.

Copyright © 2025 by
National Learning Corporation

212 Michael Drive, Syosset, NY 11791
(516) 921-8888 • www.passbooks.com
E-mail: info@passbooks.com

PASSBOOK® SERIES

THE *PASSBOOK® SERIES* has been created to prepare applicants and candidates for the ultimate academic battlefield – the examination room.

At some time in our lives, each and every one of us may be required to take an examination – for validation, matriculation, admission, qualification, registration, certification, or licensure.

Based on the assumption that every applicant or candidate has met the basic formal educational standards, has taken the required number of courses, and read the necessary texts, the *PASSBOOK® SERIES* furnishes the one special preparation which may assure passing with confidence, instead of failing with insecurity. Examination questions – together with answers – are furnished as the basic vehicle for study so that the mysteries of the examination and its compounding difficulties may be eliminated or diminished by a sure method.

This book is meant to help you pass your examination provided that you qualify and are serious in your objective.

The entire field is reviewed through the huge store of content information which is succinctly presented through a provocative and challenging approach – the question-and-answer method.

A climate of success is established by furnishing the correct answers at the end of each test.

You soon learn to recognize types of questions, forms of questions, and patterns of questioning. You may even begin to anticipate expected outcomes.

You perceive that many questions are repeated or adapted so that you can gain acute insights, which may enable you to score many sure points.

You learn how to confront new questions, or types of questions, and to attack them confidently and work out the correct answers.

You note objectives and emphases, and recognize pitfalls and dangers, so that you may make positive educational adjustments.

Moreover, you are kept fully informed in relation to new concepts, methods, practices, and directions in the field.

You discover that you are actually taking the examination all the time: you are preparing for the examination by "taking" an examination, not by reading extraneous and/or supererogatory textbooks.

In short, this PASSBOOK®, used directedly, should be an important factor in helping you to pass your test.

CIVIL ENGINEERING DRAFTSMAN

DUTIES AND RESPONSIBILITIES
Under direct supervision, performs civil engineering drafting work of ordinary difficulty and responsibility; performs related work.

EXAMPLES OF TYPICAL TASKS
Assists in research, investigations, studies or examinations related to the engineering functions or activities of a department or agency. Assists in the preparation of maps, plans, drawings, specifications and estimates of quantities. Makes, traces, inks and letters drawings, of acceptable standard quality. Performs advanced mathematical calculations and assists in the development and application of scientific formulae and scientific research. May be responsible for the indexing, accessioning and filing of maps, plans and drawings.

TESTS
The written test is expected to consist of multiple-choice questions on drafting and elementary civil engineering.

HOW TO TAKE A TEST

I. YOU MUST PASS AN EXAMINATION

A. *WHAT EVERY CANDIDATE SHOULD KNOW*

Examination applicants often ask us for help in preparing for the written test. What can I study in advance? What kinds of questions will be asked? How will the test be given? How will the papers be graded?

As an applicant for a civil service examination, you may be wondering about some of these things. Our purpose here is to suggest effective methods of advance study and to describe civil service examinations.

Your chances for success on this examination can be increased if you know how to prepare. Those "pre-examination jitters" can be reduced if you know what to expect. You can even experience an adventure in good citizenship if you know why civil service exams are given.

B. *WHY ARE CIVIL SERVICE EXAMINATIONS GIVEN?*

Civil service examinations are important to you in two ways. As a citizen, you want public jobs filled by employees who know how to do their work. As a job seeker, you want a fair chance to compete for that job on an equal footing with other candidates. The best-known means of accomplishing this two-fold goal is the competitive examination.

Exams are widely publicized throughout the nation. They may be administered for jobs in federal, state, city, municipal, town or village governments or agencies.

Any citizen may apply, with some limitations, such as the age or residence of applicants. Your experience and education may be reviewed to see whether you meet the requirements for the particular examination. When these requirements exist, they are reasonable and applied consistently to all applicants. Thus, a competitive examination may cause you some uneasiness now, but it is your privilege and safeguard.

C. *HOW ARE CIVIL SERVICE EXAMS DEVELOPED?*

Examinations are carefully written by trained technicians who are specialists in the field known as "psychological measurement," in consultation with recognized authorities in the field of work that the test will cover. These experts recommend the subject matter areas or skills to be tested; only those knowledges or skills important to your success on the job are included. The most reliable books and source materials available are used as references. Together, the experts and technicians judge the difficulty level of the questions.

Test technicians know how to phrase questions so that the problem is clearly stated. Their ethics do not permit "trick" or "catch" questions. Questions may have been tried out on sample groups, or subjected to statistical analysis, to determine their usefulness.

Written tests are often used in combination with performance tests, ratings of training and experience, and oral interviews. All of these measures combine to form the best-known means of finding the right person for the right job.

II. HOW TO PASS THE WRITTEN TEST

A. NATURE OF THE EXAMINATION

To prepare intelligently for civil service examinations, you should know how they differ from school examinations you have taken. In school you were assigned certain definite pages to read or subjects to cover. The examination questions were quite detailed and usually emphasized memory. Civil service exams, on the other hand, try to discover your present ability to perform the duties of a position, plus your potentiality to learn these duties. In other words, a civil service exam attempts to predict how successful you will be. Questions cover such a broad area that they cannot be as minute and detailed as school exam questions.

In the public service similar kinds of work, or positions, are grouped together in one "class." This process is known as *position-classification*. All the positions in a class are paid according to the salary range for that class. One class title covers all of these positions, and they are all tested by the same examination.

B. FOUR BASIC STEPS

1) Study the announcement

How, then, can you know what subjects to study? Our best answer is: "Learn as much as possible about the class of positions for which you've applied." The exam will test the knowledge, skills and abilities needed to do the work.

Your most valuable source of information about the position you want is the official exam announcement. This announcement lists the training and experience qualifications. Check these standards and apply only if you come reasonably close to meeting them.

The brief description of the position in the examination announcement offers some clues to the subjects which will be tested. Think about the job itself. Review the duties in your mind. Can you perform them, or are there some in which you are rusty? Fill in the blank spots in your preparation.

Many jurisdictions preview the written test in the exam announcement by including a section called "Knowledge and Abilities Required," "Scope of the Examination," or some similar heading. Here you will find out specifically what fields will be tested.

2) Review your own background

Once you learn in general what the position is all about, and what you need to know to do the work, ask yourself which subjects you already know fairly well and which need improvement. You may wonder whether to concentrate on improving your strong areas or on building some background in your fields of weakness. When the announcement has specified "some knowledge" or "considerable knowledge," or has used adjectives like "beginning principles of…" or "advanced … methods," you can get a clue as to the number and difficulty of questions to be asked in any given field. More questions, and hence broader coverage, would be included for those subjects which are more important in the work. Now weigh your strengths and weaknesses against the job requirements and prepare accordingly.

3) Determine the level of the position

Another way to tell how intensively you should prepare is to understand the level of the job for which you are applying. Is it the entering level? In other words, is this the position in which beginners in a field of work are hired? Or is it an intermediate or advanced level? Sometimes this is indicated by such words as "Junior" or "Senior" in the class title. Other jurisdictions use Roman numerals to designate the level – Clerk I, Clerk II, for example. The word "Supervisor" sometimes appears in the title. If the level is not indicated by the title, check the description of duties. Will you be working under very close supervision, or will you have responsibility for independent decisions in this work?

4) Choose appropriate study materials

Now that you know the subjects to be examined and the relative amount of each subject to be covered, you can choose suitable study materials. For beginning level jobs, or even advanced ones, if you have a pronounced weakness in some aspect of your training, read a modern, standard textbook in that field. Be sure it is up to date and has general coverage. Such books are normally available at your library, and the librarian will be glad to help you locate one. For entry-level positions, questions of appropriate difficulty are chosen – neither highly advanced questions, nor those too simple. Such questions require careful thought but not advanced training.

If the position for which you are applying is technical or advanced, you will read more advanced, specialized material. If you are already familiar with the basic principles of your field, elementary textbooks would waste your time. Concentrate on advanced textbooks and technical periodicals. Think through the concepts and review difficult problems in your field.

These are all general sources. You can get more ideas on your own initiative, following these leads. For example, training manuals and publications of the government agency which employs workers in your field can be useful, particularly for technical and professional positions. A letter or visit to the government department involved may result in more specific study suggestions, and certainly will provide you with a more definite idea of the exact nature of the position you are seeking.

III. KINDS OF TESTS

Tests are used for purposes other than measuring knowledge and ability to perform specified duties. For some positions, it is equally important to test ability to make adjustments to new situations or to profit from training. In others, basic mental abilities not dependent on information are essential. Questions which test these things may not appear as pertinent to the duties of the position as those which test for knowledge and information. Yet they are often highly important parts of a fair examination. For very general questions, it is almost impossible to help you direct your study efforts. What we can do is to point out some of the more common of these general abilities needed in public service positions and describe some typical questions.

1) General information

Broad, general information has been found useful for predicting job success in some kinds of work. This is tested in a variety of ways, from vocabulary lists to questions about current events. Basic background in some field of work, such as sociology or economics, may be sampled in a group of questions. Often these are principles which have become familiar to most persons through exposure rather than through formal training. It is difficult to advise you how to study for these questions; being alert to the world around you is our best suggestion.

2) Verbal ability

An example of an ability needed in many positions is verbal or language ability. Verbal ability is, in brief, the ability to use and understand words. Vocabulary and grammar tests are typical measures of this ability. Reading comprehension or paragraph interpretation questions are common in many kinds of civil service tests. You are given a paragraph of written material and asked to find its central meaning.

3) Numerical ability

Number skills can be tested by the familiar arithmetic problem, by checking paired lists of numbers to see which are alike and which are different, or by interpreting charts and graphs. In the latter test, a graph may be printed in the test booklet which you are asked to use as the basis for answering questions.

4) Observation

A popular test for law-enforcement positions is the observation test. A picture is shown to you for several minutes, then taken away. Questions about the picture test your ability to observe both details and larger elements.

5) Following directions

In many positions in the public service, the employee must be able to carry out written instructions dependably and accurately. You may be given a chart with several columns, each column listing a variety of information. The questions require you to carry out directions involving the information given in the chart.

6) Skills and aptitudes

Performance tests effectively measure some manual skills and aptitudes. When the skill is one in which you are trained, such as typing or shorthand, you can practice. These tests are often very much like those given in business school or high school courses. For many of the other skills and aptitudes, however, no short-time preparation can be made. Skills and abilities natural to you or that you have developed throughout your lifetime are being tested.

Many of the general questions just described provide all the data needed to answer the questions and ask you to use your reasoning ability to find the answers. Your best preparation for these tests, as well as for tests of facts and ideas, is to be at your physical and mental best. You, no doubt, have your own methods of getting into an exam-taking mood and keeping "in shape." The next section lists some ideas on this subject.

IV. KINDS OF QUESTIONS

Only rarely is the "essay" question, which you answer in narrative form, used in civil service tests. Civil service tests are usually of the short-answer type. Full instructions for answering these questions will be given to you at the examination. But in case this is your first experience with short-answer questions and separate answer sheets, here is what you need to know:

1) Multiple-choice Questions

Most popular of the short-answer questions is the "multiple choice" or "best answer" question. It can be used, for example, to test for factual knowledge, ability to solve problems or judgment in meeting situations found at work.

A multiple-choice question is normally one of three types—
- It can begin with an incomplete statement followed by several possible endings. You are to find the one ending which *best* completes the statement, although some of the others may not be entirely wrong.
- It can also be a complete statement in the form of a question which is answered by choosing one of the statements listed.

- It can be in the form of a problem – again you select the best answer.

Here is an example of a multiple-choice question with a discussion which should give you some clues as to the method for choosing the right answer:

When an employee has a complaint about his assignment, the action which will *best* help him overcome his difficulty is to
- A. discuss his difficulty with his coworkers
- B. take the problem to the head of the organization
- C. take the problem to the person who gave him the assignment
- D. say nothing to anyone about his complaint

In answering this question, you should study each of the choices to find which is best. Consider choice "A" – Certainly an employee may discuss his complaint with fellow employees, but no change or improvement can result, and the complaint remains unresolved. Choice "B" is a poor choice since the head of the organization probably does not know what assignment you have been given, and taking your problem to him is known as "going over the head" of the supervisor. The supervisor, or person who made the assignment, is the person who can clarify it or correct any injustice. Choice "C" is, therefore, correct. To say nothing, as in choice "D," is unwise. Supervisors have and interest in knowing the problems employees are facing, and the employee is seeking a solution to his problem.

2) True/False Questions

The "true/false" or "right/wrong" form of question is sometimes used. Here a complete statement is given. Your job is to decide whether the statement is right or wrong.

SAMPLE: A roaming cell-phone call to a nearby city costs less than a non-roaming call to a distant city.

This statement is wrong, or false, since roaming calls are more expensive.

This is not a complete list of all possible question forms, although most of the others are variations of these common types. You will always get complete directions for answering questions. Be sure you understand *how* to mark your answers – ask questions until you do.

V. RECORDING YOUR ANSWERS

Computer terminals are used more and more today for many different kinds of exams.
For an examination with very few applicants, you may be told to record your answers in the test booklet itself. Separate answer sheets are much more common. If this separate answer sheet is to be scored by machine – and this is often the case – it is highly important that you mark your answers correctly in order to get credit.

An electronic scoring machine is often used in civil service offices because of the speed with which papers can be scored. Machine-scored answer sheets must be marked with a pencil, which will be given to you. This pencil has a high graphite content which responds to the electronic scoring machine. As a matter of fact, stray dots may register as answers, so do not let your pencil rest on the answer sheet while you are pondering the correct answer. Also, if your pencil lead breaks or is otherwise defective, ask for another.

Since the answer sheet will be dropped in a slot in the scoring machine, be careful not to bend the corners or get the paper crumpled.

The answer sheet normally has five vertical columns of numbers, with 30 numbers to a column. These numbers correspond to the question numbers in your test booklet. After each number, going across the page are four or five pairs of dotted lines. These short dotted lines have small letters or numbers above them. The first two pairs may also have a "T" or "F" above the letters. This indicates that the first two pairs only are to be used if the questions are of the true-false type. If the questions are multiple choice, disregard the "T" and "F" and pay attention only to the small letters or numbers.

Answer your questions in the manner of the sample that follows:

32. The largest city in the United States is
    A. Washington, D.C.
    B. New York City
    C. Chicago
    D. Detroit
    E. San Francisco

1) Choose the answer you think is best. (New York City is the largest, so "B" is correct.)
2) Find the row of dotted lines numbered the same as the question you are answering. (Find row number 32)
3) Find the pair of dotted lines corresponding to the answer. (Find the pair of lines under the mark "B.")
4) Make a solid black mark between the dotted lines.

VI. BEFORE THE TEST

Common sense will help you find procedures to follow to get ready for an examination. Too many of us, however, overlook these sensible measures. Indeed, nervousness and fatigue have been found to be the most serious reasons why applicants fail to do their best on civil service tests. Here is a list of reminders:

- Begin your preparation early – Don't wait until the last minute to go scurrying around for books and materials or to find out what the position is all about.
- Prepare continuously – An hour a night for a week is better than an all-night cram session. This has been definitely established. What is more, a night a week for a month will return better dividends than crowding your study into a shorter period of time.
- Locate the place of the exam – You have been sent a notice telling you when and where to report for the examination. If the location is in a different town or otherwise unfamiliar to you, it would be well to inquire the best route and learn something about the building.
- Relax the night before the test – Allow your mind to rest. Do not study at all that night. Plan some mild recreation or diversion; then go to bed early and get a good night's sleep.
- Get up early enough to make a leisurely trip to the place for the test – This way unforeseen events, traffic snarls, unfamiliar buildings, etc. will not upset you.
- Dress comfortably – A written test is not a fashion show. You will be known by number and not by name, so wear something comfortable.

- Leave excess paraphernalia at home – Shopping bags and odd bundles will get in your way. You need bring only the items mentioned in the official notice you received; usually everything you need is provided. Do not bring reference books to the exam. They will only confuse those last minutes and be taken away from you when in the test room.
- Arrive somewhat ahead of time – If because of transportation schedules you must get there very early, bring a newspaper or magazine to take your mind off yourself while waiting.
- Locate the examination room – When you have found the proper room, you will be directed to the seat or part of the room where you will sit. Sometimes you are given a sheet of instructions to read while you are waiting. Do not fill out any forms until you are told to do so; just read them and be prepared.
- Relax and prepare to listen to the instructions
- If you have any physical problem that may keep you from doing your best, be sure to tell the test administrator. If you are sick or in poor health, you really cannot do your best on the exam. You can come back and take the test some other time.

VII. AT THE TEST

The day of the test is here and you have the test booklet in your hand. The temptation to get going is very strong. Caution! There is more to success than knowing the right answers. You must know how to identify your papers and understand variations in the type of short-answer question used in this particular examination. Follow these suggestions for maximum results from your efforts:

1) Cooperate with the monitor

The test administrator has a duty to create a situation in which you can be as much at ease as possible. He will give instructions, tell you when to begin, check to see that you are marking your answer sheet correctly, and so on. He is not there to guard you, although he will see that your competitors do not take unfair advantage. He wants to help you do your best.

2) Listen to all instructions

Don't jump the gun! Wait until you understand all directions. In most civil service tests you get more time than you need to answer the questions. So don't be in a hurry. Read each word of instructions until you clearly understand the meaning. Study the examples, listen to all announcements and follow directions. Ask questions if you do not understand what to do.

3) Identify your papers

Civil service exams are usually identified by number only. You will be assigned a number; you must not put your name on your test papers. Be sure to copy your number correctly. Since more than one exam may be given, copy your exact examination title.

4) Plan your time

Unless you are told that a test is a "speed" or "rate of work" test, speed itself is usually not important. Time enough to answer all the questions will be provided, but this does not mean that you have all day. An overall time limit has been set. Divide the total time (in minutes) by the number of questions to determine the approximate time you have for each question.

5) Do not linger over difficult questions

If you come across a difficult question, mark it with a paper clip (useful to have along) and come back to it when you have been through the booklet. One caution if you do this – be sure to skip a number on your answer sheet as well. Check often to be sure that you have not lost your place and that you are marking in the row numbered the same as the question you are answering.

6) Read the questions

Be sure you know what the question asks! Many capable people are unsuccessful because they failed to *read* the questions correctly.

7) Answer all questions

Unless you have been instructed that a penalty will be deducted for incorrect answers, it is better to guess than to omit a question.

8) Speed tests

It is often better NOT to guess on speed tests. It has been found that on timed tests people are tempted to spend the last few seconds before time is called in marking answers at random – without even reading them – in the hope of picking up a few extra points. To discourage this practice, the instructions may warn you that your score will be "corrected" for guessing. That is, a penalty will be applied. The incorrect answers will be deducted from the correct ones, or some other penalty formula will be used.

9) Review your answers

If you finish before time is called, go back to the questions you guessed or omitted to give them further thought. Review other answers if you have time.

10) Return your test materials

If you are ready to leave before others have finished or time is called, take ALL your materials to the monitor and leave quietly. Never take any test material with you. The monitor can discover whose papers are not complete, and taking a test booklet may be grounds for disqualification.

VIII. EXAMINATION TECHNIQUES

1) Read the general instructions carefully. These are usually printed on the first page of the exam booklet. As a rule, these instructions refer to the timing of the examination; the fact that you should not start work until the signal and must stop work at a signal, etc. If there are any *special* instructions, such as a choice of questions to be answered, make sure that you note this instruction carefully.

2) When you are ready to start work on the examination, that is as soon as the signal has been given, read the instructions to each question booklet, underline any key words or phrases, such as *least, best, outline, describe* and the like. In this way you will tend to answer as requested rather than discover on reviewing your paper that you *listed without describing*, that you selected the *worst* choice rather than the *best* choice, etc.

3) If the examination is of the objective or multiple-choice type – that is, each question will also give a series of possible answers: A, B, C or D, and you are called upon to select the best answer and write the letter next to that answer on your answer paper – it is advisable to start answering each question in turn. There may be anywhere from 50 to 100 such questions in the three or four hours allotted and you can see how much time would be taken if you read through all the questions before beginning to answer any. Furthermore, if you come across a question or group of questions which you know would be difficult to answer, it would undoubtedly affect your handling of all the other questions.

4) If the examination is of the essay type and contains but a few questions, it is a moot point as to whether you should read all the questions before starting to answer any one. Of course, if you are given a choice – say five out of seven and the like – then it is essential to read all the questions so you can eliminate the two that are most difficult. If, however, you are asked to answer all the questions, there may be danger in trying to answer the easiest one first because you may find that you will spend too much time on it. The best technique is to answer the first question, then proceed to the second, etc.

5) Time your answers. Before the exam begins, write down the time it started, then add the time allowed for the examination and write down the time it must be completed, then divide the time available somewhat as follows:
   - If 3-1/2 hours are allowed, that would be 210 minutes. If you have 80 objective-type questions, that would be an average of 2-1/2 minutes per question. Allow yourself no more than 2 minutes per question, or a total of 160 minutes, which will permit about 50 minutes to review.
   - If for the time allotment of 210 minutes there are 7 essay questions to answer, that would average about 30 minutes a question. Give yourself only 25 minutes per question so that you have about 35 minutes to review.

6) The most important instruction is to *read each question* and make sure you know what is wanted. The second most important instruction is to *time yourself properly* so that you answer every question. The third most important instruction is to *answer every question*. Guess if you have to but include something for each question. Remember that you will receive no credit for a blank and will probably receive some credit if you write something in answer to an essay question. If you guess a letter – say "B" for a multiple-choice question – you may have guessed right. If you leave a blank as an answer to a multiple-choice question, the examiners may respect your feelings but it will not add a point to your score. Some exams may penalize you for wrong answers, so in such cases *only*, you may not want to guess unless you have some basis for your answer.

7) Suggestions
   a. Objective-type questions
      1. Examine the question booklet for proper sequence of pages and questions
      2. Read all instructions carefully
      3. Skip any question which seems too difficult; return to it after all other questions have been answered
      4. Apportion your time properly; do not spend too much time on any single question or group of questions

5. Note and underline key words – *all, most, fewest, least, best, worst, same, opposite*, etc.
6. Pay particular attention to negatives
7. Note unusual option, e.g., unduly long, short, complex, different or similar in content to the body of the question
8. Observe the use of "hedging" words – *probably, may, most likely*, etc.
9. Make sure that your answer is put next to the same number as the question
10. Do not second-guess unless you have good reason to believe the second answer is definitely more correct
11. Cross out original answer if you decide another answer is more accurate; do not erase until you are ready to hand your paper in
12. Answer all questions; guess unless instructed otherwise
13. Leave time for review

b. Essay questions
1. Read each question carefully
2. Determine exactly what is wanted. Underline key words or phrases.
3. Decide on outline or paragraph answer
4. Include many different points and elements unless asked to develop any one or two points or elements
5. Show impartiality by giving pros and cons unless directed to select one side only
6. Make and write down any assumptions you find necessary to answer the questions
7. Watch your English, grammar, punctuation and choice of words
8. Time your answers; don't crowd material

8) Answering the essay question

Most essay questions can be answered by framing the specific response around several key words or ideas. Here are a few such key words or ideas:

M's: manpower, materials, methods, money, management
P's: purpose, program, policy, plan, procedure, practice, problems, pitfalls, personnel, public relations

a. Six basic steps in handling problems:
1. Preliminary plan and background development
2. Collect information, data and facts
3. Analyze and interpret information, data and facts
4. Analyze and develop solutions as well as make recommendations
5. Prepare report and sell recommendations
6. Install recommendations and follow up effectiveness

b. Pitfalls to avoid
1. *Taking things for granted* – A statement of the situation does not necessarily imply that each of the elements is necessarily true; for example, a complaint may be invalid and biased so that all that can be taken for granted is that a complaint has been registered

2. *Considering only one side of a situation* – Wherever possible, indicate several alternatives and then point out the reasons you selected the best one
3. *Failing to indicate follow up* – Whenever your answer indicates action on your part, make certain that you will take proper follow-up action to see how successful your recommendations, procedures or actions turn out to be
4. *Taking too long in answering any single question* – Remember to time your answers properly

IX. AFTER THE TEST

Scoring procedures differ in detail among civil service jurisdictions although the general principles are the same. Whether the papers are hand-scored or graded by machine we have described, they are nearly always graded by number. That is, the person who marks the paper knows only the number – never the name – of the applicant. Not until all the papers have been graded will they be matched with names. If other tests, such as training and experience or oral interview ratings have been given, scores will be combined. Different parts of the examination usually have different weights. For example, the written test might count 60 percent of the final grade, and a rating of training and experience 40 percent. In many jurisdictions, veterans will have a certain number of points added to their grades.

After the final grade has been determined, the names are placed in grade order and an eligible list is established. There are various methods for resolving ties between those who get the same final grade – probably the most common is to place first the name of the person whose application was received first. Job offers are made from the eligible list in the order the names appear on it. You will be notified of your grade and your rank as soon as all these computations have been made. This will be done as rapidly as possible.

People who are found to meet the requirements in the announcement are called "eligibles." Their names are put on a list of eligible candidates. An eligible's chances of getting a job depend on how high he stands on this list and how fast agencies are filling jobs from the list.

When a job is to be filled from a list of eligibles, the agency asks for the names of people on the list of eligibles for that job. When the civil service commission receives this request, it sends to the agency the names of the three people highest on this list. Or, if the job to be filled has specialized requirements, the office sends the agency the names of the top three persons who meet these requirements from the general list.

The appointing officer makes a choice from among the three people whose names were sent to him. If the selected person accepts the appointment, the names of the others are put back on the list to be considered for future openings.

That is the rule in hiring from all kinds of eligible lists, whether they are for typist, carpenter, chemist, or something else. For every vacancy, the appointing officer has his choice of any one of the top three eligibles on the list. This explains why the person whose name is on top of the list sometimes does not get an appointment when some of the persons lower on the list do. If the appointing officer chooses the second or third eligible, the No. 1 eligible does not get a job at once, but stays on the list until he is appointed or the list is terminated.

X. HOW TO PASS THE INTERVIEW TEST

The examination for which you applied requires an oral interview test. You have already taken the written test and you are now being called for the interview test – the final part of the formal examination.

You may think that it is not possible to prepare for an interview test and that there are no procedures to follow during an interview. Our purpose is to point out some things you can do in advance that will help you and some good rules to follow and pitfalls to avoid while you are being interviewed.

What is an interview supposed to test?

The written examination is designed to test the technical knowledge and competence of the candidate; the oral is designed to evaluate intangible qualities, not readily measured otherwise, and to establish a list showing the relative fitness of each candidate – as measured against his competitors – for the position sought. Scoring is not on the basis of "right" and "wrong," but on a sliding scale of values ranging from "not passable" to "outstanding." As a matter of fact, it is possible to achieve a relatively low score without a single "incorrect" answer because of evident weakness in the qualities being measured.

Occasionally, an examination may consist entirely of an oral test – either an individual or a group oral. In such cases, information is sought concerning the technical knowledges and abilities of the candidate, since there has been no written examination for this purpose. More commonly, however, an oral test is used to supplement a written examination.

Who conducts interviews?

The composition of oral boards varies among different jurisdictions. In nearly all, a representative of the personnel department serves as chairman. One of the members of the board may be a representative of the department in which the candidate would work. In some cases, "outside experts" are used, and, frequently, a businessman or some other representative of the general public is asked to serve. Labor and management or other special groups may be represented. The aim is to secure the services of experts in the appropriate field.

However the board is composed, it is a good idea (and not at all improper or unethical) to ascertain in advance of the interview who the members are and what groups they represent. When you are introduced to them, you will have some idea of their backgrounds and interests, and at least you will not stutter and stammer over their names.

What should be done before the interview?

While knowledge about the board members is useful and takes some of the surprise element out of the interview, there is other preparation which is more substantive. It *is* possible to prepare for an oral interview – in several ways:

1) Keep a copy of your application and review it carefully before the interview

This may be the only document before the oral board, and the starting point of the interview. Know what education and experience you have listed there, and the sequence and dates of all of it. Sometimes the board will ask you to review the highlights of your experience for them; you should not have to hem and haw doing it.

2) Study the class specification and the examination announcement

Usually, the oral board has one or both of these to guide them. The qualities, characteristics or knowledges required by the position sought are stated in these documents. They offer valuable clues as to the nature of the oral interview. For example, if the job involves supervisory responsibilities, the announcement will usually indicate that knowledge of modern supervisory methods and the qualifications of the candidate as a supervisor will be tested. If so, you can expect such questions, frequently in the form of a hypothetical situation which you are expected to solve. NEVER go into an oral without knowledge of the duties and responsibilities of the job you seek.

3) Think through each qualification required

Try to visualize the kind of questions you would ask if you were a board member. How well could you answer them? Try especially to appraise your own knowledge and background in each area, *measured against the job sought*, and identify any areas in which you are weak. Be critical and realistic – do not flatter yourself.

4) Do some general reading in areas in which you feel you may be weak

For example, if the job involves supervision and your past experience has NOT, some general reading in supervisory methods and practices, particularly in the field of human relations, might be useful. Do NOT study agency procedures or detailed manuals. The oral board will be testing your understanding and capacity, not your memory.

5) Get a good night's sleep and watch your general health and mental attitude

You will want a clear head at the interview. Take care of a cold or any other minor ailment, and of course, no hangovers.

What should be done on the day of the interview?

Now comes the day of the interview itself. Give yourself plenty of time to get there. Plan to arrive somewhat ahead of the scheduled time, particularly if your appointment is in the fore part of the day. If a previous candidate fails to appear, the board might be ready for you a bit early. By early afternoon an oral board is almost invariably behind schedule if there are many candidates, and you may have to wait. Take along a book or magazine to read, or your application to review, but leave any extraneous material in the waiting room when you go in for your interview. In any event, relax and compose yourself.

The matter of dress is important. The board is forming impressions about you – from your experience, your manners, your attitude, and your appearance. Give your personal appearance careful attention. Dress your best, but not your flashiest. Choose conservative, appropriate clothing, and be sure it is immaculate. This is a business interview, and your appearance should indicate that you regard it as such. Besides, being well groomed and properly dressed will help boost your confidence.

Sooner or later, someone will call your name and escort you into the interview room. *This is it.* From here on you are on your own. It is too late for any more preparation. But remember, you asked for this opportunity to prove your fitness, and you are here because your request was granted.

What happens when you go in?

The usual sequence of events will be as follows: The clerk (who is often the board stenographer) will introduce you to the chairman of the oral board, who will introduce you to the other members of the board. Acknowledge the introductions before you sit down. Do not be surprised if you find a microphone facing you or a stenotypist sitting by. Oral interviews are usually recorded in the event of an appeal or other review.

Usually the chairman of the board will open the interview by reviewing the highlights of your education and work experience from your application – primarily for the benefit of the other members of the board, as well as to get the material into the record. Do not interrupt or comment unless there is an error or significant misinterpretation; if that is the case, do not hesitate. But do not quibble about insignificant matters. Also, he will usually ask you some question about your education, experience or your present job – partly to get you to start talking and to establish the interviewing "rapport." He may start the actual questioning, or turn it over to one of the other members. Frequently, each member undertakes the questioning on a particular area, one in which he is perhaps most competent, so you can expect each member to participate in the examination. Because time is limited, you may also expect some rather abrupt switches in the direction the questioning takes, so do not be upset by it. Normally, a board member will not pursue a single line of questioning unless he discovers a particular strength or weakness.

After each member has participated, the chairman will usually ask whether any member has any further questions, then will ask you if you have anything you wish to add. Unless you are expecting this question, it may floor you. Worse, it may start you off on an extended, extemporaneous speech. The board is not usually seeking more information. The question is principally to offer you a last opportunity to present further qualifications or to indicate that you have nothing to add. So, if you feel that a significant qualification or characteristic has been overlooked, it is proper to point it out in a sentence or so. Do not compliment the board on the thoroughness of their examination – they have been sketchy, and you know it. If you wish, merely say, "No thank you, I have nothing further to add." This is a point where you can "talk yourself out" of a good impression or fail to present an important bit of information. Remember, *you close the interview yourself.*

The chairman will then say, "That is all, Mr. _____, thank you." Do not be startled; the interview is over, and quicker than you think. Thank him, gather your belongings and take your leave. Save your sigh of relief for the other side of the door.

How to put your best foot forward
Throughout this entire process, you may feel that the board individually and collectively is trying to pierce your defenses, seek out your hidden weaknesses and embarrass and confuse you. Actually, this is not true. They are obliged to make an appraisal of your qualifications for the job you are seeking, and they want to see you in your best light. Remember, they must interview all candidates and a non-cooperative candidate may become a failure in spite of their best efforts to bring out his qualifications. Here are 15 suggestions that will help you:

1) Be natural – Keep your attitude confident, not cocky
If you are not confident that you can do the job, do not expect the board to be. Do not apologize for your weaknesses, try to bring out your strong points. The board is interested in a positive, not negative, presentation. Cockiness will antagonize any board member and make him wonder if you are covering up a weakness by a false show of strength.

2) Get comfortable, but don't lounge or sprawl
Sit erectly but not stiffly. A careless posture may lead the board to conclude that you are careless in other things, or at least that you are not impressed by the importance of the occasion. Either conclusion is natural, even if incorrect. Do not fuss with your clothing, a pencil or an ashtray. Your hands may occasionally be useful to emphasize a point; do not let them become a point of distraction.

3) Do not wisecrack or make small talk
This is a serious situation, and your attitude should show that you consider it as such. Further, the time of the board is limited – they do not want to waste it, and neither should you.

4) Do not exaggerate your experience or abilities

In the first place, from information in the application or other interviews and sources, the board may know more about you than you think. Secondly, you probably will not get away with it. An experienced board is rather adept at spotting such a situation, so do not take the chance.

5) If you know a board member, do not make a point of it, yet do not hide it

Certainly you are not fooling him, and probably not the other members of the board. Do not try to take advantage of your acquaintanceship – it will probably do you little good.

6) Do not dominate the interview

Let the board do that. They will give you the clues – do not assume that you have to do all the talking. Realize that the board has a number of questions to ask you, and do not try to take up all the interview time by showing off your extensive knowledge of the answer to the first one.

7) Be attentive

You only have 20 minutes or so, and you should keep your attention at its sharpest throughout. When a member is addressing a problem or question to you, give him your undivided attention. Address your reply principally to him, but do not exclude the other board members.

8) Do not interrupt

A board member may be stating a problem for you to analyze. He will ask you a question when the time comes. Let him state the problem, and wait for the question.

9) Make sure you understand the question

Do not try to answer until you are sure what the question is. If it is not clear, restate it in your own words or ask the board member to clarify it for you. However, do not haggle about minor elements.

10) Reply promptly but not hastily

A common entry on oral board rating sheets is "candidate responded readily," or "candidate hesitated in replies." Respond as promptly and quickly as you can, but do not jump to a hasty, ill-considered answer.

11) Do not be peremptory in your answers

A brief answer is proper – but do not fire your answer back. That is a losing game from your point of view. The board member can probably ask questions much faster than you can answer them.

12) Do not try to create the answer you think the board member wants

He is interested in what kind of mind you have and how it works – not in playing games. Furthermore, he can usually spot this practice and will actually grade you down on it.

13) Do not switch sides in your reply merely to agree with a board member

Frequently, a member will take a contrary position merely to draw you out and to see if you are willing and able to defend your point of view. Do not start a debate, yet do not surrender a good position. If a position is worth taking, it is worth defending.

14) Do not be afraid to admit an error in judgment if you are shown to be wrong

The board knows that you are forced to reply without any opportunity for careful consideration. Your answer may be demonstrably wrong. If so, admit it and get on with the interview.

15) Do not dwell at length on your present job

The opening question may relate to your present assignment. Answer the question but do not go into an extended discussion. You are being examined for a *new* job, not your present one. As a matter of fact, try to phrase ALL your answers in terms of the job for which you are being examined.

Basis of Rating

Probably you will forget most of these "do's" and "don'ts" when you walk into the oral interview room. Even remembering them all will not ensure you a passing grade. Perhaps you did not have the qualifications in the first place. But remembering them will help you to put your best foot forward, without treading on the toes of the board members.

Rumor and popular opinion to the contrary notwithstanding, an oral board wants you to make the best appearance possible. They know you are under pressure – but they also want to see how you respond to it as a guide to what your reaction would be under the pressures of the job you seek. They will be influenced by the degree of poise you display, the personal traits you show and the manner in which you respond.

ABOUT THIS BOOK

This book contains tests divided into Examination Sections. Go through each test, answering every question in the margin. We have also attached a sample answer sheet at the back of the book that can be removed and used. At the end of each test look at the answer key and check your answers. On the ones you got wrong, look at the right answer choice and learn. Do not fill in the answers first. Do not memorize the questions and answers, but understand the answer and principles involved. On your test, the questions will likely be different from the samples. Questions are changed and new ones added. If you understand these past questions you should have success with any changes that arise. Tests may consist of several types of questions. We have additional books on each subject should more study be advisable or necessary for you. Finally, the more you study, the better prepared you will be. This book is intended to be the last thing you study before you walk into the examination room. Prior study of relevant texts is also recommended. NLC publishes some of these in our Fundamental Series. Knowledge and good sense are important factors in passing your exam. Good luck also helps. So now study this Passbook, absorb the material contained within and take that knowledge into the examination. Then do your best to pass that exam.

EXAMINATION SECTION

EXAMINATION SECTION

TEST 1

DIRECTIONS: Each question or incomplete statement is followed by several suggested answers or completions. Select the one that BEST answers the question or completes the statement. *PRINT THE LETTER OF THE CORRECT ANSWER IN THE SPACE AT THE RIGHT.*

1. A minimum of _____ orthographic view(s) is(are) required to show the three dimensions of any object and, therefore, to describe its shape completely.
   A. one   B. two   C. three   D. four

   1._____

2. In isometric projections, the angle between any two of the coordinates is _____ degrees.
   A. 30   B. 90   C. 120   D. 60

   2._____

3. The thickness of an object line is equal to _____ mm on the A4 paper size.
   A. 0.5   B. 0.25   C. 0.45   D. 0.75

   3._____

4. ANSI stands for
   A. American National Standards Institute
   B. AutoCad Notations Systematic Index
   C. All-purpose Notations Systematic Index
   D. American National Standards Index

   4._____

5. Based on ANSI standards, a parts list should be located in the _____ corner above the title block.
   A. upper right   B. lower right   C. lower left   D. lower top right

   5._____

6. A mirror tool in CAD software requires _____ to create the reversed reflected object.
   A. point of surface   B. line of surface
   C. line of reflection   D. axis of surface

   6._____

7. In model space, everything is drawn at a scale of _____ to one.
   A. one   B. two   C. three   D. one and a half

   7._____

8. Hidden lines are not
   A. curved   B. edged   C. doubled   D. dimensioned

   8._____

9. Countersink drilling is indicated by a _____-shaped symbol in CAD.
   A. cross   B. V   C. U   D. square

   9._____

10. Computer-aided-designing technologies allow you to add _____ properties to the designs.
    A. mass   B. dimensional   C. transitional   D. conventional

    10._____

11. _____ feature-based modeling means that 3D geometry is created by adding or removing material with known dimensions.
    A. Parametric   B. Mass   C. Dimensioned   D. CAD

12. American computer-aided drawings use _____ -angle projections.
    A. first   B. second   C. third   D. fourth

13. BOM stands for
    A. Bill of Material
    B. Bill of Mass
    C. Body of Material
    D. Batch of Material

14. To convert a 2D sketch into a 3D model, the designer needs to add _____ to the sketch.
    A. width   B. area   C. mass   D. height

15. Dimensions shown in brackets are called _____ dimensions.
    A. functional   B. discrete   C. mutual   D. auxiliary

16. The diameter of the shaft is an example of _____ dimension.
    A. functional   B. discrete   C. mutual   D. auxiliary

17. There is(are) _____ main classification(s) of dimensions in an engineering drawing.
    A. one   B. two   C. three   D. four

18. Extrude command does not work if your 2D geometry is not
    A. closed   B. angular   C. symmetrical   D. proportional

19. Cone shape can be created with the help of the extrude-_____ command.
    A. taper   B. remove   C. plunge   D. loft

20. A sloped-roof CAD model is an example of which of the following CAD commands?
    A. Extrude-loft
    B. Extrude-taper
    C. Extrude-remove
    D. Extrude-cone

21. The sweep command needs a minimum of _____ input variable(s) to develop a sweep 3D structure.
    A. one   B. two   C. three   D. four

22. The helix command can be executed with one diameter input and _____ in the structure.
    A. number of turns
    B. one radial input
    C. pitch
    D. length

23. The loft command requires a minimum of _____ planner structure(s) to create a 3D model.
    A. one   B. two   C. three   D. four

24. Multiple cross-sections
    A. can be selected in the shell command
    B. cannot be selected in the shell command
    C. can be selected in the shell command, depending on the software tool
    D. can be selected in the shell command, depending on the default plane

25. Boolean tools in CAD software do not allow
    A. removing the overlapping material from the geometry
    B. combining the two geometries
    C. surfacing the structure
    D. sweeping the structure

KEY (CORRECT ANSWERS)

1.	B	11.	A
2.	C	12.	C
3.	A	13.	A
4.	A	14.	D
5.	B	15.	D
6.	C	16.	A
7.	A	17.	C
8.	D	18.	A
9.	B	19.	A
10.	A	20.	B

21.	B
22.	A
23.	B
24.	A
25.	D

TEST 2

DIRECTIONS: Each question or incomplete statement is followed by several suggested answers or completions. Select the one that BEST answers the question or completes the statement. *PRINT THE LETTER OF THE CORRECT ANSWER IN THE SPACE AT THE RIGHT.*

1. CAD is the _____ step for computer-aided finite element analysis.   1._____
   A. first   B. second   C. third   D. last

2. Chamfer command requires _____ input to perform the operation.   2._____
   A. distance   B. diameter   C. area   D. radius

3. Chamfer command can also be performed using a _____ operation in 3D modeling software.   3._____
   A. Boolean   B. sweep   C. reverse   D. radial

4. Modeling features cannot be added on the   4._____
   A. wireframes   B. viewports   C. assemblies   D. shells

5. If the surface demands special treatments (e.g., to be covered by wear-resistance material, special lacquer, etc.), this has to be shown on the CAD drawing.   5._____
   A. This statement is universally true
   B. This statement is universally false
   C. This depends on the drafter
   D. This depends on drawing standards

6. In a CAD assembly, all parts are named by their _____ numbers.   6._____
   A. BOM   B. company   C. dimension   D. part

7. A(n) _____ assembly CAD model is created to show how the parts are joined together.   7._____
   A. sectioned   B. colored   C. orthogonal   D. projected

8. Title block does not contain which of the following information?   8._____
   A. Name of drafter   B. Sheet number
   C. Estimated weight   D. CAD software

9. Projection theory is NOT based on the   9._____
   A. line of sight   B. angle of sight
   C. plane of sight   D. size of the plane

10. Scale 1:A shows _____ of the drawing by factor A.   10._____
    A. section   B. reduction   C. division   D. addition

11. Elbow pipe shaft can be drawn with the help of   11._____
    A. loft   B. sweep   C. extrude   D. taper

12. CAD rules allow symbolizing the structures in drawing. 12.____
    A. This statement is universally true
    B. This statement is universally false
    C. This is only allowed for highly complex parts
    D. This depends on drawing standards

13. Hidden lines represent features that cannot be seen in the 13.____
    A. current view   B. CAD view
    C. parallel projection   D. perpendicular projection

14. DIN is a _____ technical standard. 14.____
    A. Danish   B. German   C. Japanese   D. British

15. Revisions and modifications in a CAD print are mentioned on the _____ 15.____
    corner.
    A. upper right   B. lower right   C. lower left   D. lower top right

16. A polyline is a connected sequent of line segments and acts as 16.____
    A. a single object   B. multiple lines
    C. a closed geometry   D. an open geometry

17. A 3D model of a fidget spinner is an example of a _____ command. 17.____
    A. pattern   B. sweep   C. chamfer   D. polyline

18. A 2D sketch of a screw can be converted to 3D model in CAD with the help of 18.____
    a _____ command.
    A. helix   B. revolve cut   C. pattern   D. sweep

19. To create a 3D dome, the shape of a 2D cross-section should be a 19.____
    A. semi-circle   B. circle   C. quad circle   D. sphere

20. In a CAD assembly, a minimum of _____ part(s) must be completely fixed 20.____
    in the model space.
    A. one   B. two   C. three   D. zero

21. In a CAD assembly, the structure is constraint in the _____ plane. 21.____
    A. default   B. front   C. perpendicular   D. first

22. Changing the part dimension in parametric modeling _____ of its associated 22.____
    parts.
    A. will not change the dimensions
    B. will change the dimensions
    C. will change the mass properties and the dimensions
    D. will not change the mass properties and the dimensions

23. Explicit modeling is _____ of parametric feature based modeling. 23.____
    A. a type   B. not a type   C. an extension   D. a tool

24. The drawing must include the _____ required to accurately manufacture the design.
    A. mass calculations
    B. number of dimensions
    C. tooling types
    D. manufacturing nomenclature

25. Rib structure cannot be drawn _____ the sketch plane.
    A. parallel to
    B. perpendicular to
    C. opposite to
    D. revolving

KEY (CORRECT ANSWERS)

1.	A	11.	B
2.	A	12.	C
3.	A	13.	A
4.	A	14.	B
5.	A	15.	A
6.	D	16.	A
7.	A	17.	A
8.	D	18.	B
9.	D	19.	C
10.	B	20.	A

21. A
22. C
23. B
24. B
25. C

EXAMINATION SECTION
TEST 1

DIRECTIONS: Each question or incomplete statement is followed by several suggested answers of completions. Select the one that BEST answers the question or complete the statement. PRINT THE LETTER OF THE CORRECT ANSWER IN THE SPACE AT THE RIGHT.

1. Three point perspective drawing has _____ converging point(s).   1._____
   A. 1
   B. 2
   C. 3
   D. 4

2. In structural drafting, section lines are used to represent   2._____
   A. cross sectional cuts
   B. hidden features
   C. hidden planes
   D. cross sectional theoretical cuts

3. Which of the following is purely a draft file format?   3._____
   A. .dwg
   B. .igs
   C. .iges
   D. .stl

4. In third angle projections, the plane of projection is   4._____
   A. no projection plane
   B. in between the observer and object
   C. below the object
   D. before the observer

5. Architectural "A" size sheet has the dimensions of   5._____
   A. Size = 8 x 11
   B. Size = 8-1/2 x 11-1/2
   C. Size = 8-1/2 x 11
   D. Size = 8 x 11

6. Bilateral means two _____.   6._____
   A. edges
   B. sides
   C. corners
   D. radii

7. Symbol of "BOM" on a draft means   7._____
   A. base of material
   B. bills of manufacturing
   C. budget of manufacturing
   D. bill of material

8. Changing from 2D to 3D in CAD means
    A. changing drawing standards
    B. giving height to planer sketch
    C. changing lengths
    D. changing software settings

9. DIN is a _____ CAD standard.
    A. British
    B. SI
    C. German
    D. Japanese

10. Workplanes in CAD software are the same as
    A. cross sections
    B. sketches
    C. drafting layers
    D. floors

11. In CAD software, trim command is part of a _____ panel.
    A. sketch
    B. draw
    C. modify
    D. it is available in all panels

12. Tapering function in CAD requires
    A. draft plane
    B. draft direction
    C. either draft plane or draft direction
    D. both draft plane and draft direction

13. Copilot snapping refers to a change in which of the following?
    A. Line color and thickness
    B. Cursor color and shape
    C. Screen color and shape
    D. Layer color and thickness

14. CADD software offers at least _____ different views of the drawing.
    A. 6
    B. 5
    C. 7
    D. 8

15. A CAM module generates the
    A. production instructions
    B. machine code
    C. manufacturing instructions
    D. G codes and M codes

16. What is the "Layer Cake Approach" in CAD?   16._____
    A. Building the part on entirely separate layers
    B. Removing the part layer by layer
    C. Splitting a part into layers
    D. Building the part by adding feature on previous layers

17. What is the basic difference between sweep and loft?   17._____
    A. Sweep is complex; loft is simple
    B. Loft is a user-dragable tool
    C. Loft can have multiple profiles
    D. Sweep can have multiple paths

18. What are the benefits of using CAD tools over traditional drawing methods?   18._____
    A. They are more efficient for the drafter
    B. Computer tools allow more proficiency and freedom
    C. They offer standardized formats
    D. All of the above

19. Pull command would be the same as   19._____
    A. revolve
    B. remove
    C. sweep
    D. extrude

20. Which one of the following is not an input parameter for radial patterns?   20._____
    A. Axis
    B. Offset
    C. Rectangular increment
    D. Shape of pattern

21. Trimetric view shows the object such that   21._____
    A. all the sides are equal
    B. all the sides are not equal
    C. all the angles are equal
    D. it provides the planer view of the object

22. Which one is preferred from a manufacturing point of view?   22._____
    A. Blend over chamfer
    B. Chamfer over blend
    C. Taper over chamfer
    D. Chamfer over blend and taper

23. Which of these is a one point command?   23._____
    A. Line
    B. Circle
    C. Arc
    D. Construction line

24. Which of the following cannot be adjusted in Initial System Settings? 24._____
    A. Drawing zones
    B. Drafting standards
    C. Draft formats
    D. All of the above

25. Self-intersecting surfaces are monitored by 25._____
    A. check manufacturing operations tool
    B. check parts tool
    C. check dimensions tool
    D. CAD software does not check this.

KEY (CORRECT ANSWERS)

1.	C	11.	C
2.	D	12.	C
3.	A	13.	B
4.	B	14.	C
5.	C	15.	D
6.	B	16.	D
7.	D	17.	C
8.	B	18.	D
9.	C	19.	D
10.	C	20.	C

21.	B
22.	B
23.	B
24.	C
25.	B

TEST 2

DIRECTIONS: Each question or incomplete statement is followed by several suggested answers of completions. Select the one that BEST answers the question or complete the statement. PRINT THE LETTER OF THE CORRECT ANSWER IN THE SPACE AT THE RIGHT.

1. Section lines can also be referred as _____ lines.
   A. hidden
   B. phantom
   C. cross section
   D. cutting

   1._____

2. Architectural "B" size sheet has the dimensions of
   A. Size = 11 x 15
   B. Size = 11 x 17
   C. Size = 17 x 11
   D. Size = 17 x 15

   2._____

3. _____ lines are not part of the main draft.
   A. Hidden
   B. Section
   C. Construction
   D. Reference

   3._____

4. Universal format for CAD is
   A. .txt
   B. .iges
   C. .stl
   D. .dwg

   4._____

5. Units, number of layers and layer styles are basically required for drawing _____.
   A. standards
   B. layouts
   C. settings
   D. format

   5._____

6. Chamfer feature in CAD can be defined by
   A. angle to face
   B. edge length
   C. either of the above
   D. both of the above

   6._____

7. What is the horizontal surface angle for isometrics drawings?
   A. 30 degrees
   B. 45 degrees
   C. 60 degrees
   D. No fixed standard

   7._____

8. _____ is the basic tool in CAD software to change a sketch in a model.
   A. Extrude
   B. Chamfer
   C. Blend
   D. Shell

9. Which of the following is the commonly followed design standard in the US?
   A. ANSI
   B. JIS
   C. DIN
   D. SI

10. What information is not conveyed by snap function?
    A. Bi section
    B. Layer
    C. End point
    D. Corner lines

11. Spline is a _____ function.
    A. linear
    B. mathematical
    C. interpolation
    D. algebraic

12. Blind hole in CAD parts is a hole
    A. drawn as a hidden feature
    B. that is not visible in front view
    C. that is not visible in top view
    D. that does not go through all of the material

13. CAD Designer can have minimum _____ different views of the drawing.
    A. 6
    B. 5
    C. 7
    D. 8

14. What is the potter's wheel approach in CAD?
    A. Revolving a 2D to make a desired model
    B. Removing material to make a desired model
    C. Using Boolean operators to make a desired model
    D. Adding material to make a desired model

15. Sweep cross section should be
    A. symmetrical
    B. normal to the path
    C. closed
    D. smaller than the path size

16. Loft is an extended form of
    A. revolve
    B. sweep
    C. taper
    D. pull

    16._____

17. What is the difference between punch command and stamp command?
    A. Punch removes material outside the profile
    B. Punch is 3D and stamp is 2D
    C. Stamp removes material outside the profile
    D. There is no difference

    17._____

18. Pull angular command would be the same as
    A. extrude angular
    B. revolve
    C. sweep
    D. helix

    18._____

19. Orthographic projection always has the same dimensions as of the dimensions of object because projection lines are
    A. parallel to plane
    B. parallel to observer
    C. perpendicular with each other
    D. perpendicular to plane

    19._____

20. Which file type is used to transfer a CAD file for CAM?
    A. .dwg
    B. .stl
    C. .env
    D. .pk

    20._____

21. What is the difference between counter-bore and counter-sink?
    A. Counter-bore increases the hole diameter conically; counter-sink increases the hole diameter cylindrically
    B. Counter-bore increases the hole diameter cylindrically; counter-sink increases the hole diameter conically
    C. Counter-bore decreases the hole diameter conically; counter-sink decreases the hole diameter cylindrically
    D. Counter-bore decreases the hole diameter conically; counter-sink increases the hole diameter conically

    21._____

22. Which of the following statements is NOT true for 3D wireframes?
    A. It is an extension of 2D drafting
    B. It is an extension of 3D modeling
    C. It has no mass properties
    D. Features cannot be directly added in it

    22._____

23. What is the function of the mate tool?
    A. Joining parts together
    B. Aligning surfaces together
    C. Position surfaces as desired
    D. All of the above

24. Trim can also be used as
    A. delete
    B. remove
    C. boolean subtract
    D. all of the above

25. Layer cake approach requires expertise in
    A. drafting
    B. modeling
    C. manufacturing
    D. assembling

KEY (CORRECT ANSWERS)

1.	B		11.	B
2.	B		12.	D
3.	C		13.	C
4.	B		14.	A
5.	C		15.	C
6.	C		16.	B
7.	A		17.	C
8.	A		18.	B
9.	A		19.	D
10.	B		20.	B

21.	B
22.	B
23.	A
24.	A
25.	B

TEST 3

DIRECTIONS: Each question or incomplete statement is followed by several suggested answers of completions. Select the one that BEST answers the question or complete the statement. PRINT THE LETTER OF THE CORRECT ANSWER IN THE SPACE AT THE RIGHT.

1. Object lines are also called _____ lines.   1._____
    A. feature
    B. visible
    C. contour
    D. fix

2. Line weight is maximum for _____ lines.   2._____
    A. centre
    B. construction
    C. hidden
    D. object

3. "TOL" symbol on an architectural draft represents   3._____
    A. tool specification
    B. tolerance
    C. tools list
    D. test organizations list

4. Architectural "C" size sheet has the dimensions of   4._____
    A. Size = 22 x 34
    B. Size = 17 x 22
    C. Size = 8-1/2 x 11
    D. Size = 11 x 17

5. Observer – Plane – Object is the orientation for _____ projections.   5._____
    A. first angle
    B. isometric
    C. third angle
    D. perspective

6. Area, number of views and orientation of views are features that define drawing   6._____
    A. standards
    B. layouts
    C. settings
    D. format

7. To draw a fillet on draft, you need to define its
   A. curvature
   B. interior radius
   C. side length
   D. exterior radius

8. What is the main difference between a "sketch" and "model" in CAD?
   A. Different standards
   B. Increased number of dimensions
   C. Increased measurements
   D. Change in the perspective of observer

9. CAD offers _____ planer views of the object.
   A. 3
   B. 4
   C. 5
   D. 6

10. What is the basic CAD tool for the "Potter's wheel" approach?
    A. Extrude
    B. Remove
    C. Sweep
    D. Revolve

11. What is the basic CAD tool for "Layer Cake" approach?
    A. Extrude
    B. Remove
    C. Sweep
    D. Revolve

12. What are the input parameters for counter-bore?
    A. Diameter and depth
    B. Diameter and angle
    C. Diameter increment and tangent direction
    D. Diameter reduction and angle

13. Orthographic projection has projection lines that are
    A. parallel to plane
    B. parallel to observer
    C. perpendicular with each other
    D. perpendicular to plane

14. Dimetric view shows the object such that
    A. any two angles are equal
    B. any two angles are equal
    C. any two sides and angles are equal
    D. any two sides and angles are unequal

15. View port does not contain
    A. features info
    B. history
    C. layers
    D. annotations

16. Which two features are the same from a manufacturing point of view?
    A. Chamfer and blend
    B. Blend and fillet
    C. Revolve and sweep
    D. Sweep and loft

17. Which statement is NOT true about CAD Boolean functions?
    A. They unite two parts
    B. They subtract two parts
    C. They find the intersecting region
    D. They can assemble the parts

18. Shell command in CAD
    A. increases the number dimensions of part
    B. increases the number of faces in part
    C. adds material to the part
    D. decreases the dimensions of part

19. Sweep command works by
    A. extrapolating the cross section on defined path
    B. extending the cross section on defined path
    C. extruding the cross section on defined path
    D. revolving the cross section on defined path

20. Dynamic positioning tools allow the user to work on _____ degrees of freedom.
    A. 3
    B. 4
    C. 5
    D. 6

21. What is not an input parameter for Helix tool?
    A. Axis
    B. Path
    C. Turns
    D. Pitch

22. Trim command is available in
    A. Sketch panel
    B. Draw panel
    C. Modify panel
    D. Model pane

23. Which statement is not true about the loft command?
    A. Loft can have multiple cross sections
    B. Loft is an extension of sweep command
    C. Loft only work on single path
    D. Loft can have multiple profiles

24. CAD tools make 3D models by
    A. mathematical parameters
    B. geometrical features
    C. structural parameters
    D. manufacturing parameters

25. Which method is preferred from a "usage" point of view?
    A. Blend over chamfer
    B. Chamfer over blend
    C. Taper over chamfer
    D. Chamfer over blend and taper

KEY (CORRECT ANSWERS)

1.	B	11.	A
2.	D	12.	A
3.	B	13.	D
4.	B	14.	C
5.	C	15.	B
6.	B	16.	B
7.	B	17.	D
8.	B	18.	B
9.	D	19.	C
10.	D	20.	D

21. B
22. C
23. C
24. B
25. A

TEST 4

DIRECTIONS: Each question or incomplete statement is followed by several suggested answers of completions. Select the one that BEST answers the question or complete the statement. PRINT THE LETTER OF THE CORRECT ANSWER IN THE SPACE AT THE RIGHT.

1. The term "Poche" is used for _____ in architectural drafts. 1._____
    A. borders
    B. material information
    C. textural patterns
    D. size information

2. To draw an architectural floor plan, which feature of CAD software is used? 2._____
    A. Annotation
    B. Layer
    C. Sketch
    D. Model

3. Architectural "D" size sheet has the dimensions of 3._____
    A. Size = 21 x 34
    B. Size = 20 x 34
    C. Size = 22 x 30
    D. Size = 22 x 34

4. Observer – Object – Plane is an example of _____ projections. 4._____
    A. first angle
    B. isometric
    C. third angle
    D. perspective

5. CAD tools are NOT used for 5._____
    A. simulations
    B. analysis
    C. HR Estimation
    D. visualization

6. ANSI stands for 6._____
    A. American National Standards Implementation
    B. American Northern Standards Institute
    C. American National Standards Institute
    D. American Nationals Standardization and Implementation

7. Which of the following software is NOT used for drafting purposes?
   A. Inventor
   B. Solid Edge
   C. Visual Studio
   D. Pro-E

8. Computerized systems represent different layers of a draft by different
   A. symbols
   B. names
   C. levels
   D. colors

9. How many degrees of freedom a CAD tool can offer to any object?
   A. 3
   B. 4
   C. 5
   D. 6

10. Sweep is an extended form of
    A. extrude
    B. revolve
    C. helix
    D. loft

11. Designers can use both layer cake and potter's wheel approach while making parts in CAD. The preferred approach will depend on
    A. complexity of the design
    B. CAD tools
    C. product requirements
    D. all of the above

12. Potter's wheel approach requires expertise in
    A. drafting
    B. modeling
    C. manufacturing
    D. assembling

13. Which of the following is true for 3D wireframes?
    A. It is an extension of 2D drafting
    B. It is an extension of 3D modeling
    C. It has same mass properties as 3D model
    D. Features can be directly added in it

14. What are the input parameters for counter-sink feature?
    A. Diameter and depth
    B. Diameter and angle
    C. Diameter increment and tangent direction
    D. Diameter reduction and angle

15. Which of the following statements is NOT true regarding punch command?
    A. Punch removes material inside the profile
    B. Punch is an extension of extrude command
    C. Stamp removes material outside the profile
    D. Punch and stamp are same

16. A slot can be defined by
    A. one center point and vertical offset
    B. two center points and vertical offset
    C. two center points and horizontal offset
    D. one center point and horizontal offset

17. Which two features are the same from a manufacturing point of view?
    A. Chamfer and blend
    B. Drill and bore
    C. Revolve and sweep
    D. Sweep and loft

18. Boolean functions allow the user to
    A. unite two parts
    B. subtract two parts
    C. find the intersecting region
    D. all of the above

19. CAD software checks for self-intersecting surfaces by
    A. check dimensions tool
    B. CAD software does not check this
    C. check manufacturing operations tool
    D. check parts tool

20. "Parent-Child" term in CAD is used for
    A. actual feature and derived feature
    B. actual part and derived part
    C. actual draft and derived draft
    D. all of the above

21. GA is the symbol for:
    A. Gain
    B. Gauge
    C. General Alignment
    D. General Annotations

22. IGES stands for:
    A. Initial Graphics Exchange Standard
    B. Initial Graphics Exchange Specification
    C. International Graphics Exchange Standards
    D. Initial Graphics Estimation Specifications

23. Mating feature in assembly tools can
    A. join parts together
    B. align surfaces together
    C. position surfaces as desired
    D. perform all of the above functions

24. Line weight is minimum for _____ lines.
    A. centre
    B. construction
    C. section
    D. object

25. For shell command in CAD, offset is
    A. uniform for all sides
    B. larger for top side
    C. larger for bottom side
    D. larger for bottom side and same for side walls

KEY (CORRECT ANSWERS)

1.	C	11.	A
2.	B	12.	A
3.	D	13.	A
4.	A	14.	B
5.	C	15.	D
6.	C	16.	C
7.	C	17.	B
8.	D	18.	D
9.	D	19.	D
10.	B	20.	D

21.	B
22.	B
23.	B
24.	B
25.	A

EXAMINATION SECTION
TEST 1

DIRECTIONS: Each question or incomplete statement is followed by several suggested answers or completions. Select the one that BEST answers the question or completes the statement. *PRINT THE LETTER OF THE CORRECT ANSWER IN THE SPACE AT THE RIGHT.*

1. A planimeter is used to determine

    A. elevations
    B. slopes of lines
    C. bearings of lines
    D. areas

    1.____

2. Of the following, the line that is drawn the heaviest on a drawing is a(n)

    A. center line of an object
    B. dimension line
    C. reference line to an object
    D. object line

    2.____

3. The scale of a drawing is one inch equals one foot. The number of inches on a drawing for an actual distance of 3'3" would be _____ inches.

    A. 3 B. 3 1/4 C. 3 1/2 D. 3 3/4

    3.____

4. The purpose of this geometric construction is to
    A. draw four similar triangles
    B. draw four parallel lines
    C. divide EG into four equal parts
    D. divide EF into four equal parts

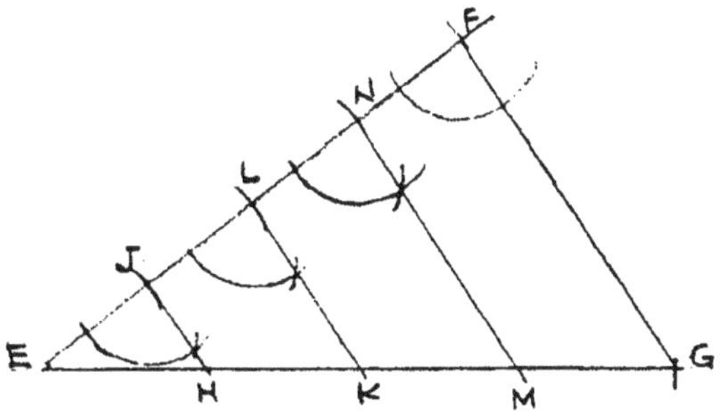

    4.____

5. In fabricating steel beams, holes are usually

    A. punched *only*
    B. punched and reamed
    C. drilled *only*
    D. drilled and reamed

    5.____

6. Of the following, the type of wood that is LEAST likely used in the construction of the frame of a wood frame house would be

    A. Douglas fir
    B. pine
    C. hemlock
    D. maple

    6.____

7. In the topographic map shown at the right, the line with the STEEPEST slope is
    A. EF
    B. EG
    C. HJ
    D. HK

    7.____

23

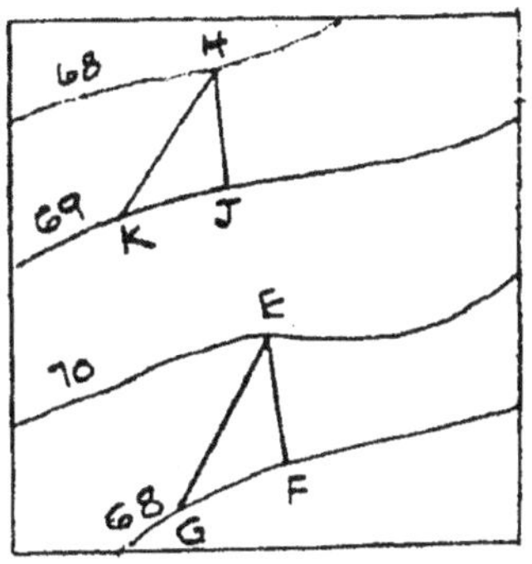

8. The number of cubic yards in a block of concrete 25' x 10' x 3' is MOST NEARLY

   A. 24   B. 26   C. 28   D. 30

9. The slope of a sewer is .0007. The change in elevation of the sewer in 1000 feet is MOST NEARLY

   A. 8 1/8"   B. 8 3/8"   C. 8 5/8"   D. 8 7/8"

10. One acre is equal to _____ square feet.

    A. 21,780   B. 32,170   C. 43,560   D. 65,340

11. The area of the rectangular piece of property that measures 8" x 4 1/2" on the drawing whose scale is 1" = 20' is _____ square feet.
    A. 3,600
    B. 7,200
    C. 10,800
    D. 14,400

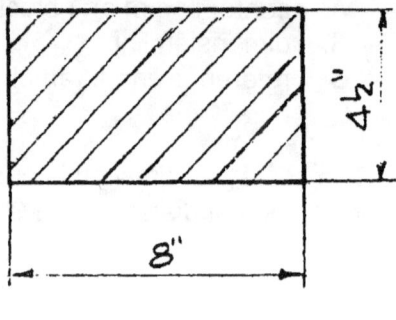

PLOT PLAN
scale 1"=20'

12. The prismoid formula for the volume of a prism whose ends are parallel is $V = h/6 (b_1+b_2+4m)$, where h is the height, b_1 is the area of the base, b_2 is the area of the top, and m is the area of the section midway between the base and the top. The volume of the prism shown at the right is MOST NEARLY
    A. 50
    B. 52
    C. 54
    D. 56

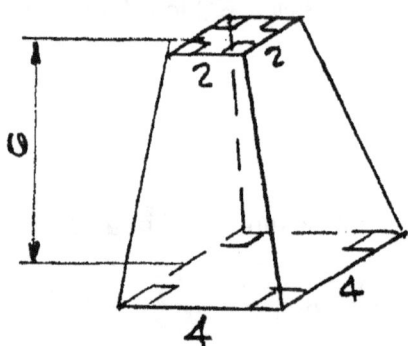

Questions 13-16.

DIRECTIONS: Questions 13 through 16 refer to the diagram below.

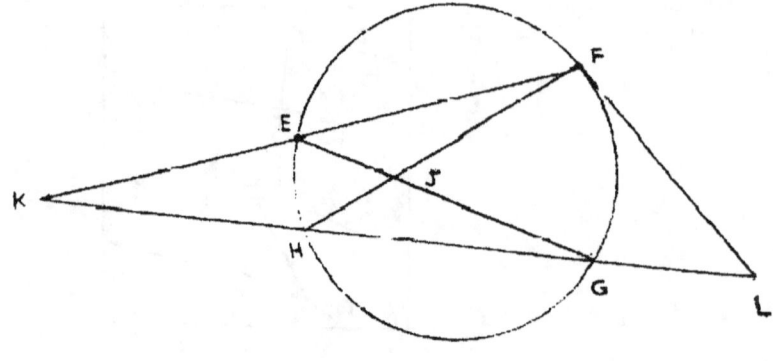

$\overarc{EF} = 120°$
$\overarc{FG} = 80°$
$\overarc{GH} = 115°$

$\overline{FL}$ is tangent to the circle at F

13. Arc EH equals   13._____
    A. 30°   B. 135°   C. 140°   D. 45°

14. Angle FEG equals   14._____
    A. 35°   B. 40°   C. 45°   D. 50°

15. Angle K equals   15._____
    A. 17 1/2°   B. 20°   C. 22 1/2°   D. 25°

16. Angle FJG equals   16._____
    A. 60°   B. 62 1/2°   C. 65°   D. 67 1/2°

Questions 17-21.

DIRECTIONS: Questions 17 through 21, inclusive, refer to the working lines of half a truss.

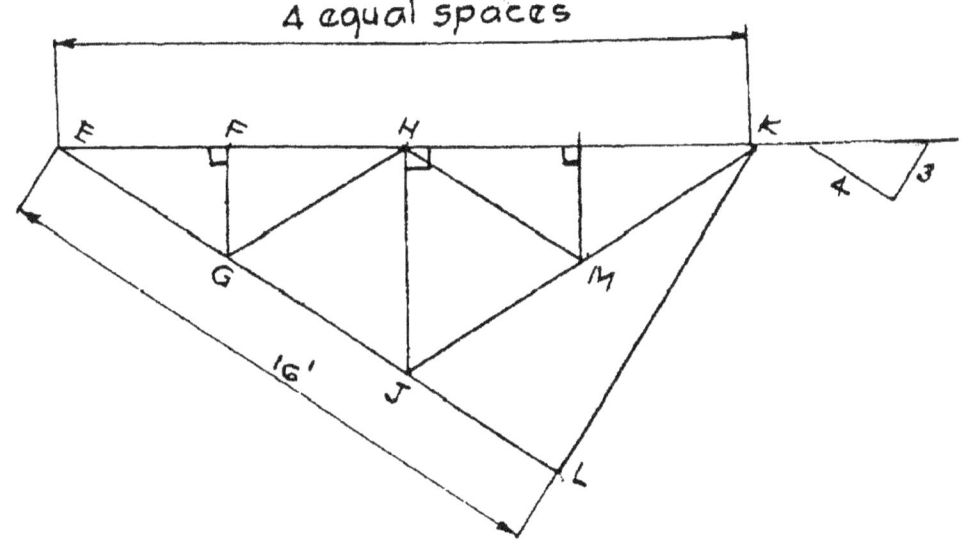

17. The length of EF is, in feet, MOST NEARLY   17._____
    A. 4.0   B. 4.5   C. 5.0   D. 5.5

18. The length of HJ is, in feet, MOST NEARLY   18._____
    A. 7.0   B. 7.5   C. 8.0   D. 8.5

19. The length of JK is, in feet, MOST NEARLY   19._____
    A. 11.0   B. 11.5   C. 12.0   D. 12.5

20. The length of KL is, in feet, MOST NEARLY   20._____
    A. 10.5   B. 11.0   C. 11.5   D. 12.0

21. The length of JL is, in feet, MOST NEARLY   21.____
    A. 5.0   B. 4.5   C. 4.0   D. 3.5

22. The cosine of angle E is   22.____
    A. 3/5
    B. 4/5
    C. 5/4
    D. 5/3

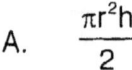

23. The sin 75° equals   23.____

    A. sin 45° cos 30° + cos 45° sin 30°
    B. sin 45° cos 30° - cos 45° sin 30°
    C. cos 45° cos 30° + sin 45° sin 30°
    D. cos 45° cos 30° - sin 45° sin 30°

24. The volume of a right cone with a radius *r* and a height *h* is   24.____

    A. $\dfrac{\pi r^2 h}{2}$ B. $\dfrac{\pi r^2 h}{3}$ C. $\dfrac{\pi r^2 h}{4}$ D. $\dfrac{\pi r^2 h}{6}$

25. The area of the triangle shown at the right, in   25.____
    square units, is
    A. 25
    B. 30
    C. 40
    D. 45

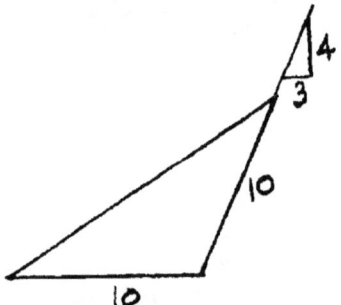

KEY (CORRECT ANSWERS)

1. D
2. D
3. B
4. C
5. A

6. D
7. A
8. C
9. B
10. C

11. D
12. D
13. D
14. B
15. A

16. B
17. C
18. B
19. D
20. D

21. D
22. B
23. A
24. B
25. C

TEST 2

DIRECTIONS: Each question or incomplete statement is followed by several suggested answers or completions. Select the one that BEST answers the question or completes the statement. *PRINT THE LETTER OF THE CORRECT ANSWER IN THE SPACE AT THE RIGHT.*

Questions 1-7.

DIRECTIONS: Questions 1 through 7, inclusive, are to be answered on the basis of the following: Given the front and top views of an object, print the letter of the CORRECT right side view.

1.

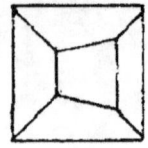

TOP VIEW

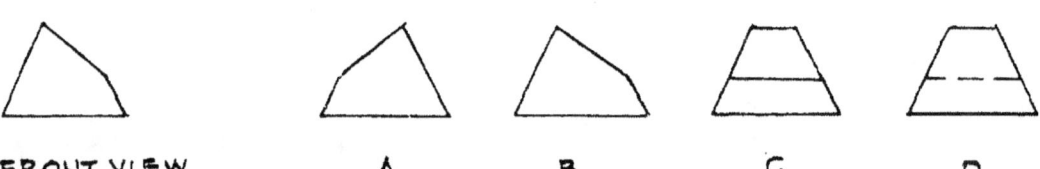

FRONT VIEW   A   B   C   D

1.____

2.

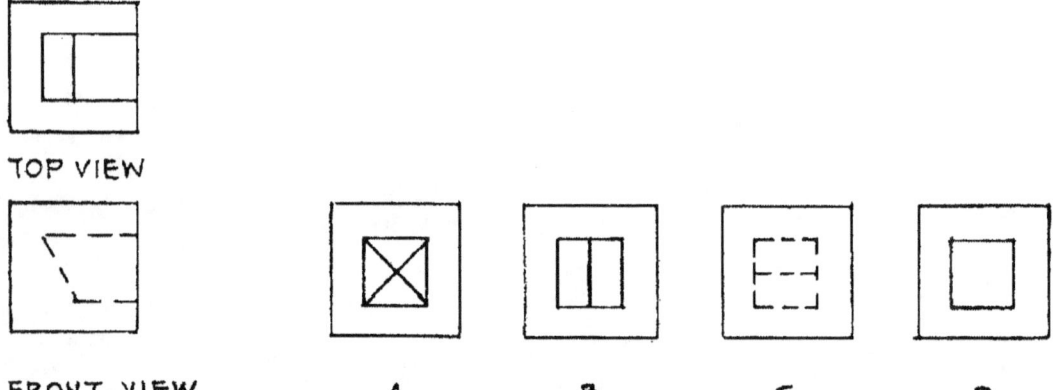

TOP VIEW

FRONT VIEW   A   B   C   D

2.____

28

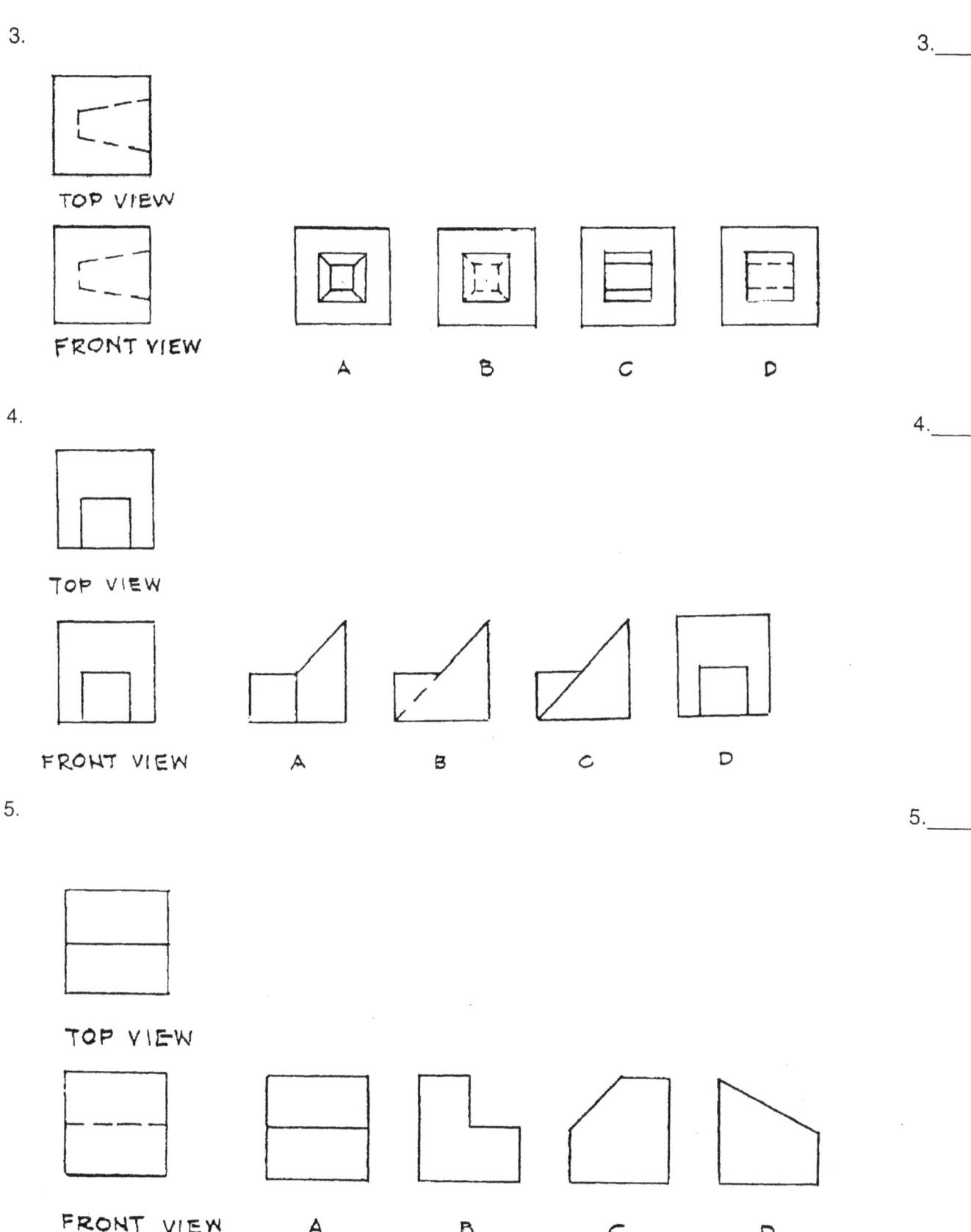

6.

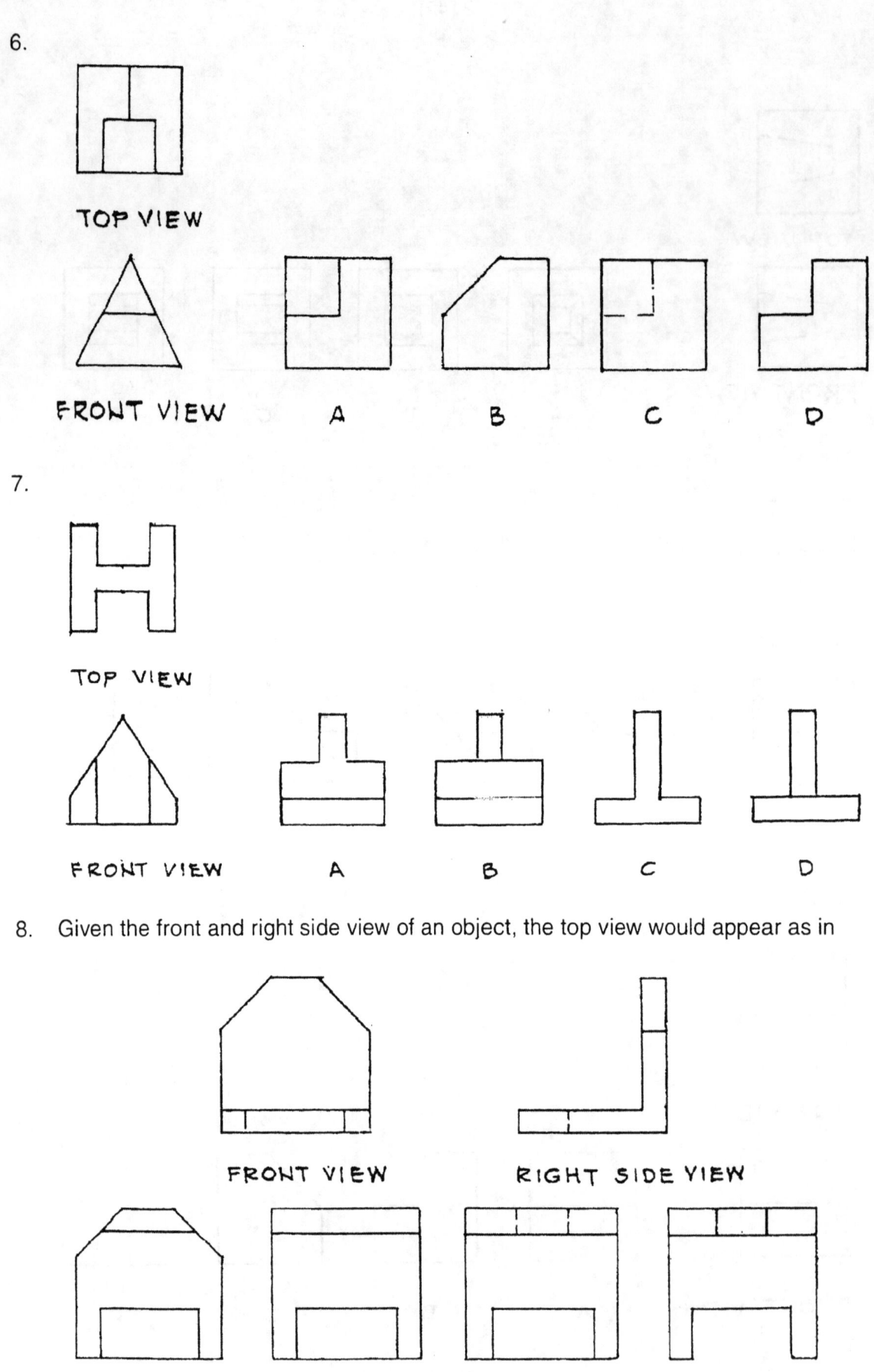

7.

8. Given the front and right side view of an object, the top view would appear as in

Questions 9-12.

DIRECTIONS: In answering Questions 9 through 12, inclusive, find the volume of each solid in cubic feet.

9.

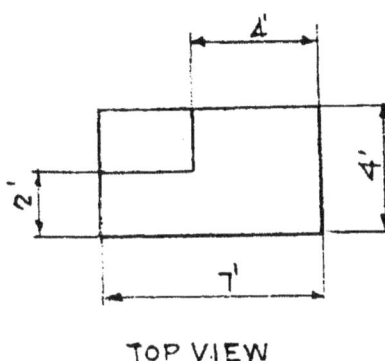

TOP VIEW

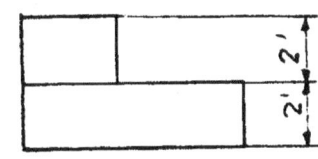

FRONT VIEW

A. 62   B. 64   C. 66   D. 68

9._____

10.

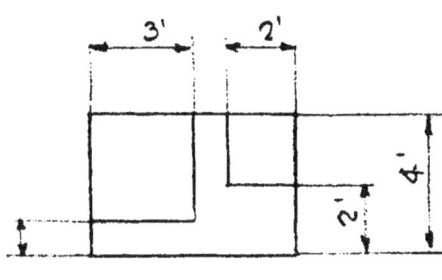

TOP VIEW

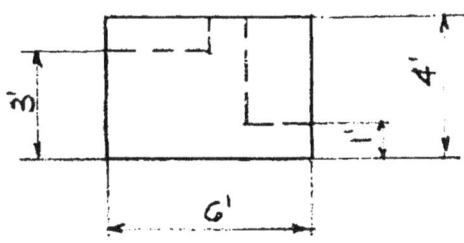

FRONT VIEW

A. 70   B. 73   C. 75   D. 77

10._____

11.

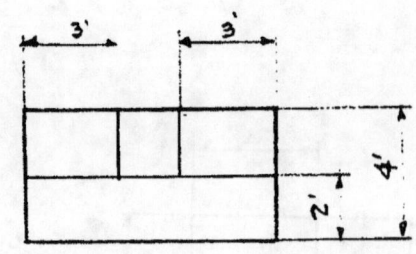

TOP VIEW

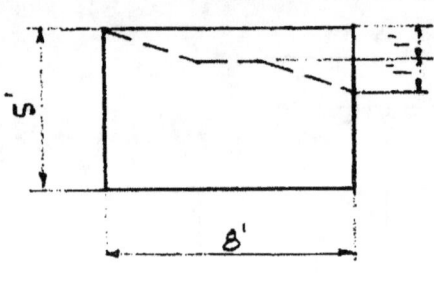

FRONT VIEW

  A. 144 B. 146 C. 148 D. 150

12.

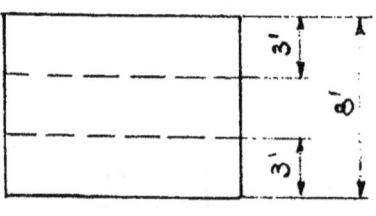

TOP VIEW

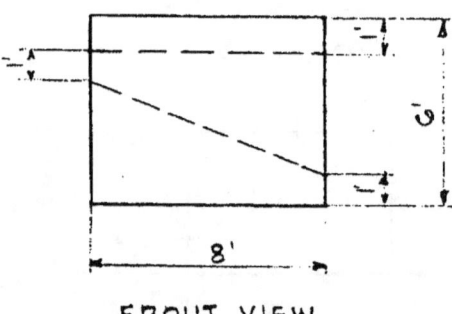

FRONT VIEW

  A. 332 B. 336 C. 340 D. 344

13. The top view would appear as in   13._____

14. The top view would appear as in   14._____

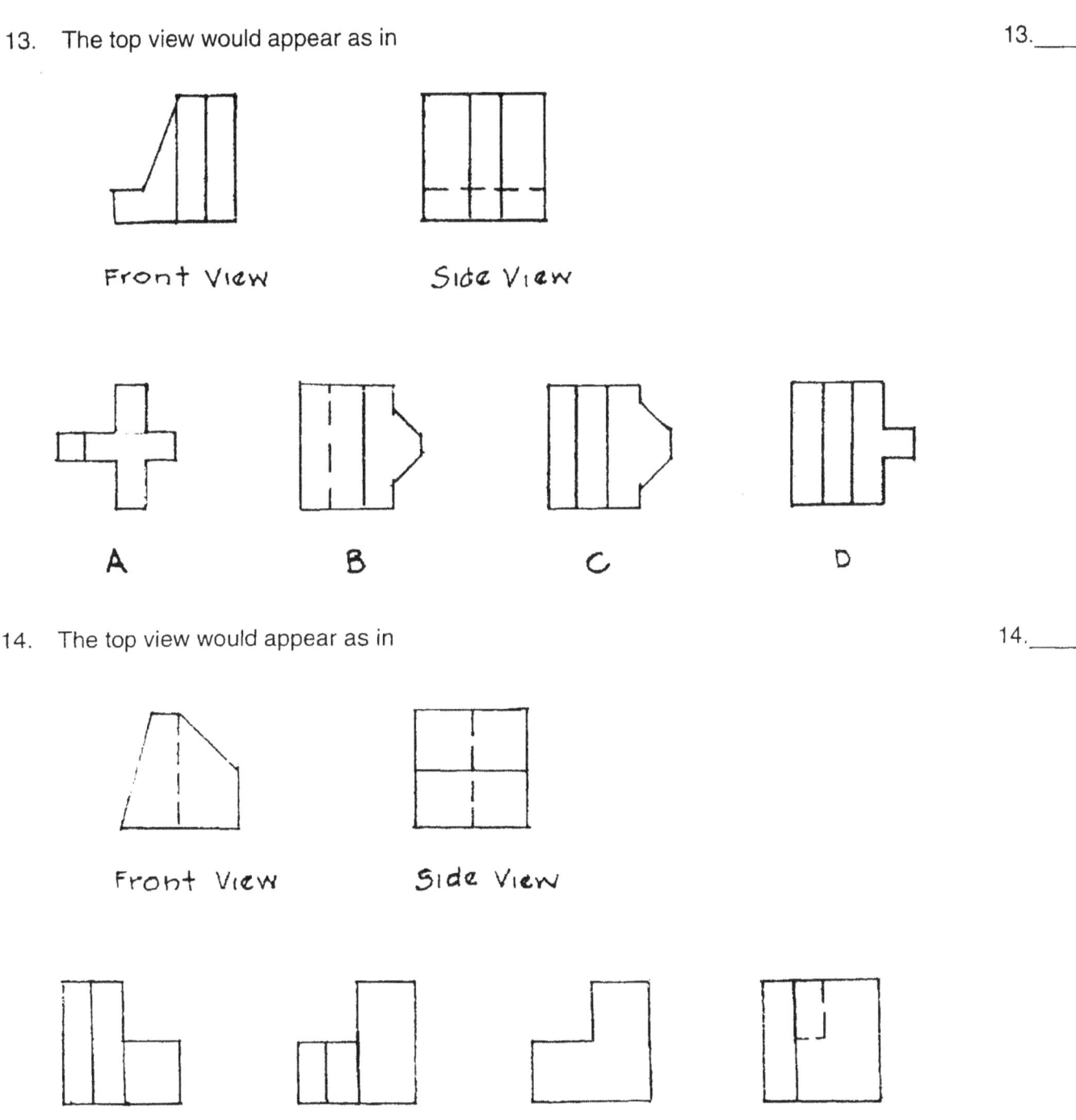

15. The top view would appear as in

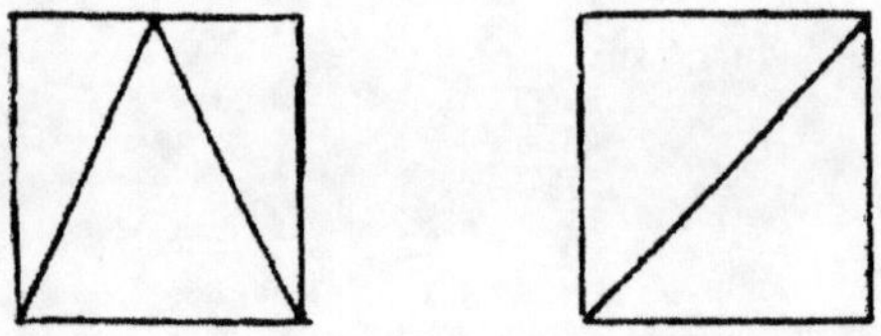

Front View   Side View

A   B   C   D

16. The top view would appear as in

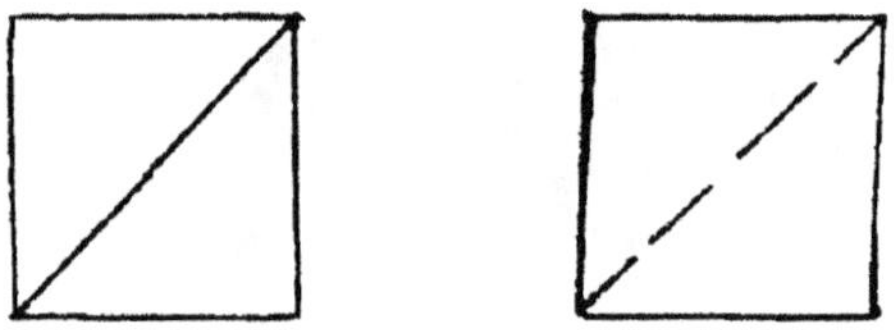

Front View   Side View

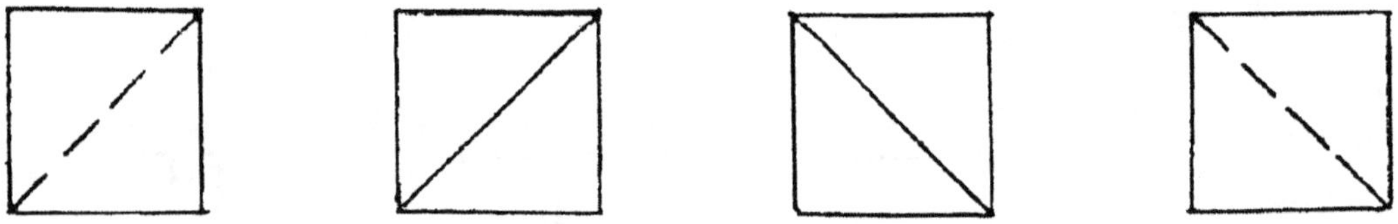

A   B   C   D

17. The top view would appear as in   17.____

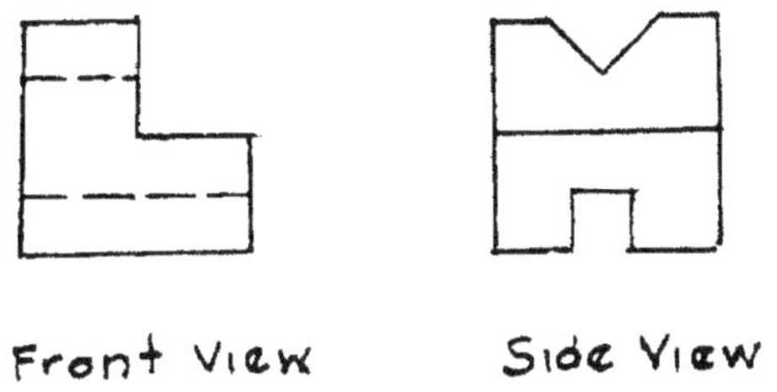

Front View   Side View

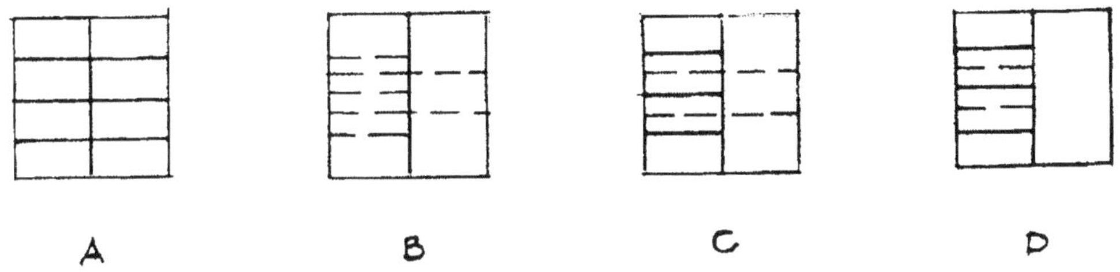

A   B   C   D

18. The top view would appear as in   18.____

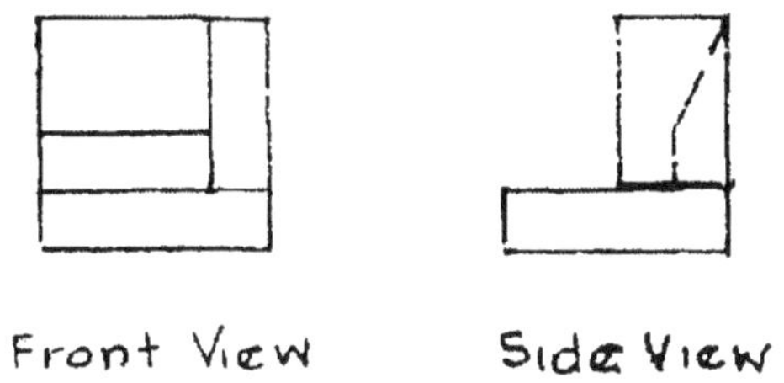

Front View   Side View

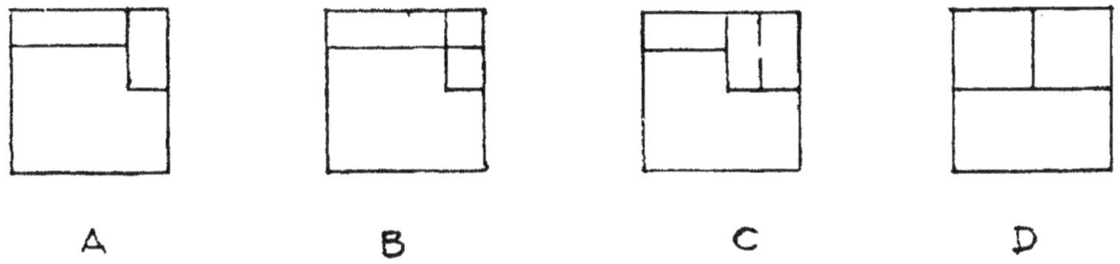

A   B   C   D

19. The symbol for steel in cross-section is

A.    B.    C. 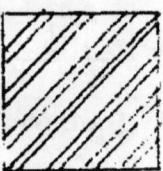   D.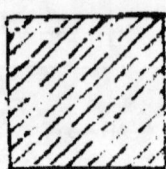

20. 1.65° is, in degrees and minutes,

    A. 1°3.9'   B. 1°39'   C. 1°0.65'   D. 1°6.5'

21. The hole shown at the right is MOST likely
    A. broached
    B. countersunk
    C. reamed
    D. counterbored

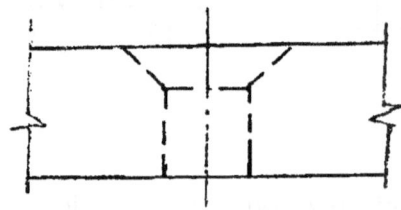

22. In isometric drawing, the isometric base line makes an angle with the horizontal equal to

    A. 30°   B. 35°   C. 40°   D. 45°

23. 1 1/8 inches is, in feet, MOST NEARLY

    A. .0833   B. .0883   C. .0938   D. .0988

24. The bearing of line OA is N30°E and the bearing of line OB is S20°E. The angle formed by the two lines is

    A. 40°   B. 50°   C. 130°   D. 150°

25. The length of the tangent EF to the circle, radius 5", centered at 0 is

    A. $5\sqrt{3}$
    B. 8
    C. $6\sqrt{2}$
    D. $\sqrt{70}$

25. ____

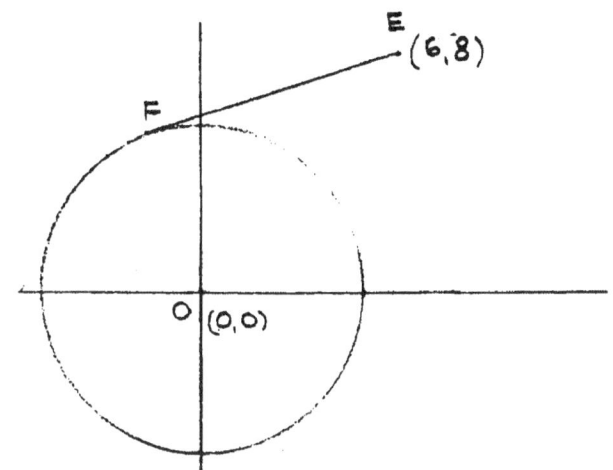

KEY (CORRECT ANSWERS)

1.	C	11.	A
2.	D	12.	D
3.	A	13.	D
4.	C	14.	B
5.	B	15.	B
6.	D	16.	C
7.	A	17.	C
8.	D	18.	A
9.	D	19.	C
10.	C	20.	B

21. B
22. A
23. C
24. C
25. A

EXAMINATION SECTION
TEST 1

DIRECTIONS: Each question or incomplete statement is followed by several suggested answers or completions. Select the one that BEST answers the question or completes the statement. *PRINT THE LETTER OF THE CORRECT ANSWER IN THE SPACE AT THE RIGHT.*

1. A rectangular solid measures 3" x 4" x 12". The diagonal of the solid is, in inches, MOST NEARLY
   A. 5   B. 9   C. 13   D. 17

   1.____

2. The area of the sector shown is, in square inches, MOST NEARLY
   A. 5
   B. 9
   C. 13
   D. 17

   2.____

3. The tangent of an acute angle of a right triangle is the ratio of the _____ side to the _____ .

   A. adjacent; opposite side
   B. opposite; hypotenuse
   C. adjacent; hypotenuse
   D. opposite; adjacent side

   3.____

4. The cross-section of each end of an excavation is shown thus:

   The length of the excavation is 81 feet. The number of cubic yards excavated is MOST NEARLY
   A. 1150   B. 1175   C. 1200   D. 1225

   4.____

5. The x,y coordinates of two points on a line are (1,2) and (3,4), respectively. The distance between the two points is MOST NEARLY
   A. 2.00   B. 2.67   C. 2.83   D. 3.00

   5.____

6. The equation y = ax + b is an equation of a(n)
   A. circle
   B. straight line
   C. ellipse
   D. parabola

   6.____

7. If one side of a triangle inscribed in a circle passes through the center of the circle, the triangle MUST be a(n) _____ triangle.
   A. isosceles
   B. isosceles right
   C. equilateral
   D. right

   7.____

8. A round steel bar 1" in diameter supports a load of 15,000#.
   The stress in the steel, in pounds per square inch, is MOST NEARLY

   A. 15,000   B. 16,300   C. 17,600   D. 19,000

9. The sine of 30° is MOST NEARLY

   A. .5   B. .75   C. 1.0   D. 1.5

10. A paved walk ten feet wide makes a 90 turn, as shown at the right. The length of the outside edge of the curve, AB, exceeds the length of the inside edge of the curve, CD, by _____ feet.

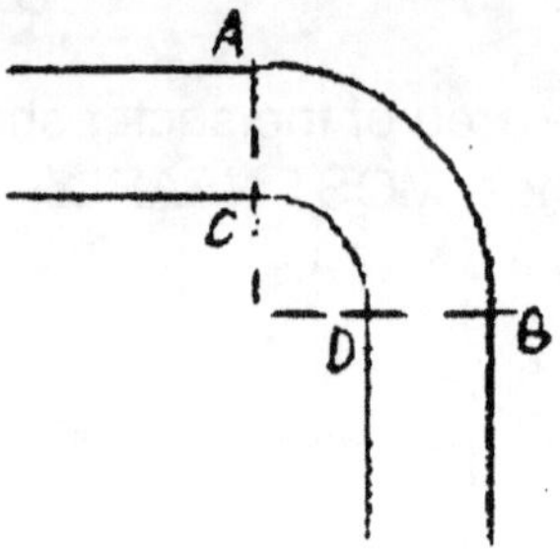

    A. 10π
    B. 5π
    C. 2π
    D. π

11. Of the following statements, the one that is CORRECT is: A

    A. Wrico pen may not be used with a Leroy guide
    B. Leroy pen may be used with either a Wrico guide or a Leroy guide
    C. Leroy pen may not be used without a guide
    D. Wrico pen may not be used without a guide

12. An instrument used exclusively for drawing equidistant cross-hatching lines is a(n)

    A. Ames guide   B. Braddock device
    C. parallel ruler   D. section liner

13. An instrument used in drawing circles of large radius is a

    A. bow compass   B. beam compass
    C. French curve   D. planimeter

14. Of the following, the one that does NOT show an object in three dimensions is a(n)

    A. perspective drawing   B. isometric drawing
    C. orthographic view   D. oblique projection

15. The head of a screw shown at the right is a _____ head.

    A. round   B. oval
    C. fillister   D. flat

16. Good drafting practice does NOT require the

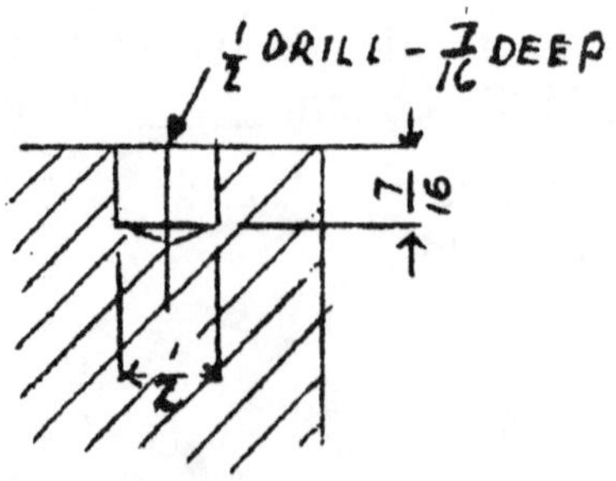

    A. 1/2 dimension
    B. 7/16 dimension
    C. 1/2 and 7/16 dimensions
    D. note: 1/2 drill -7/16 deep

17. Bevel X at end of shaft is a 17.____
    A. camber
    B. knurl
    C. taper
    D. chamfer

18. Good drafting practice requires that _____ be placed outside the figure. 18.____
    A. all dimensions
    B. the horizontal dimensions
    C. the vertical dimensions
    D. the overall dimensions

19. A dimension, $1.000 \pm {}^{.004}_{.001}$ on a detail drawing, means that the 19.____
    A. number of parts shipped may be between four more and one less than the number ordered
    B. designer is not sure what the dimension should be
    C. part is not drawn to scale
    D. size may vary

20. A sandpaper pad is useful to a draftsman for 20.____

    A. removing ink from drawing instruments
    B. sharpening pencils
    C. removing the gloss from tracing paper
    D. removing small ink projections

21. A drop pen is GENERALLY useful for drawing 21.____

    A. contour lines
    B. with a French curve as a guide
    C. small circles
    D. parallel lines

22. In good drafting practice, vertical lettering should always 22.____

    A. be avoided
    B. read from the bottom up
    C. read from the bottom up on the right side of the sheet and from the top down on the left side of the sheet
    D. read from the top down

23. To draw a line making an angle of 75° with a given line, place 23.____

    A. two triangles together so that the sum of a pair of adjacent angles is 75° and use the T-square as a guide
    B. two triangles together so that the sum of a pair of adjacent angles is 105° and use the T-square as a guide

C. two triangles together so that the sum of a pair of adjacent angles is 75° and adjust one side of the angle thus formed to the given line
D. a 30°-60° triangle on the given line and use another 30°-60° triangle for the required line

24. If a curve is to be drawn connecting two tangents, it is BEST to draw 24.____
    A. the curve first and then the tangents
    B. the tangents first and then the curve
    C. a tangent, the curve, and the second tangent in that order, from right to left
    D. a tangent, the curve, and the second tangent in that order, from left to right

25. The mark at the edge of the part shown indicates that the 25.____ 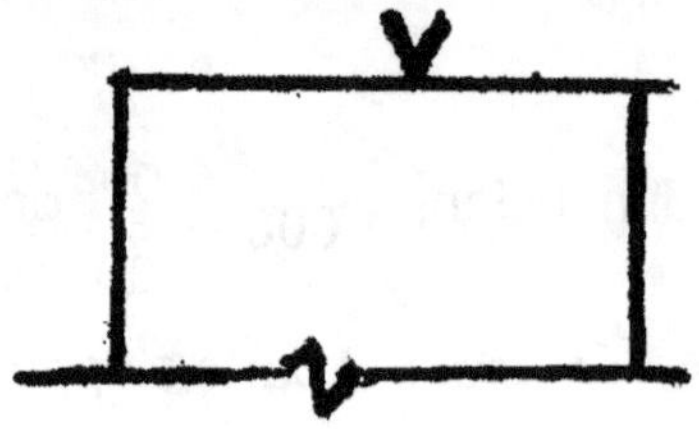
    A. surface represented by this edge is to be finished
    B. entire part is to be finished
    C. surface represented by this edge is to be welded
    D. hole drilled in the surface represented by this edge is to be countersunk

26. The symbol shown at the right represents, in section, 26.____ 
    A. plaster
    B. terra cotta
    C. brick
    D. wood

27. The symbol shown at the right represents, in section, 27.____ 
    A. steel
    B. brass
    C. aluminum
    D. cast iron

28. The symbol shown at the right represents, in section, 28.____ 
    A. rock
    B. earth
    C. sand
    D. water table

29. The symbol shown at the right represents a 29.____ 
    A. spur gear
    B. helical gear
    C. screw thread
    D. cam

30. A steel member that is shown at the right is a

    A. wide flange beam
    B. plate girder
    C. channel
    D. C-beam

31. Contour lines that are spaced far apart GENERALLY indicate a

    A. valley
    B. ridge
    C. steep grade
    D. flat grade

32. A profile is

    A. a topographic drawing
    B. the outline of a vertical section of the earth's surface
    C. a method of determining horizontal distance without actual measurement
    D. a landscape plan of a plot

33. A map is drawn to a scale of 1 inch equals 100 ft. The BEST instrument to use for scaling distances on that map is a(n)

    A. slide rule
    B. architect's scale
    C. 50 ft. tape
    D. engineer's scale

34. The bearing of a line is the

    A. influence that the line exerts on the traverse
    B. angle which the line makes with the north-south line
    C. accurately measured length of the line
    D. angle it makes with a known reference line and its length

35. A grade which has a rise of 3 ft. in 300 ft. is a grade of

    A. 1%   B. .01%   C. 3%   D. 10%

Questions 36-40.

DIRECTIONS: In each of Questions 36 through 40, the front and top views of an object are given. Of the views labeled 1, 2, 3, and 4, select the one that CORRECTLY represents the right side view of each object for third angle projection.

36.

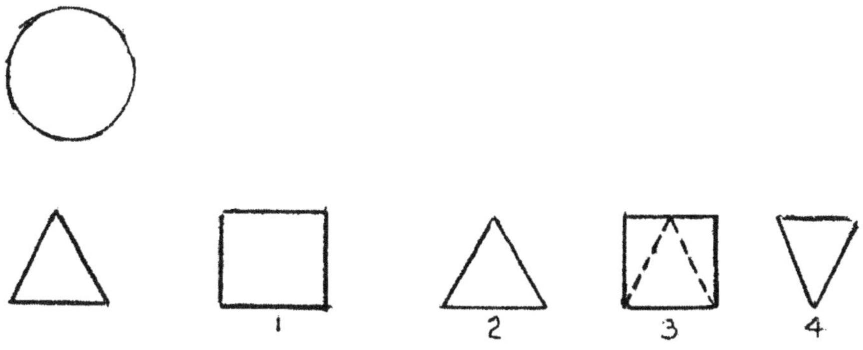

    A. 1   B. 2   C. 3   D. 4

37.

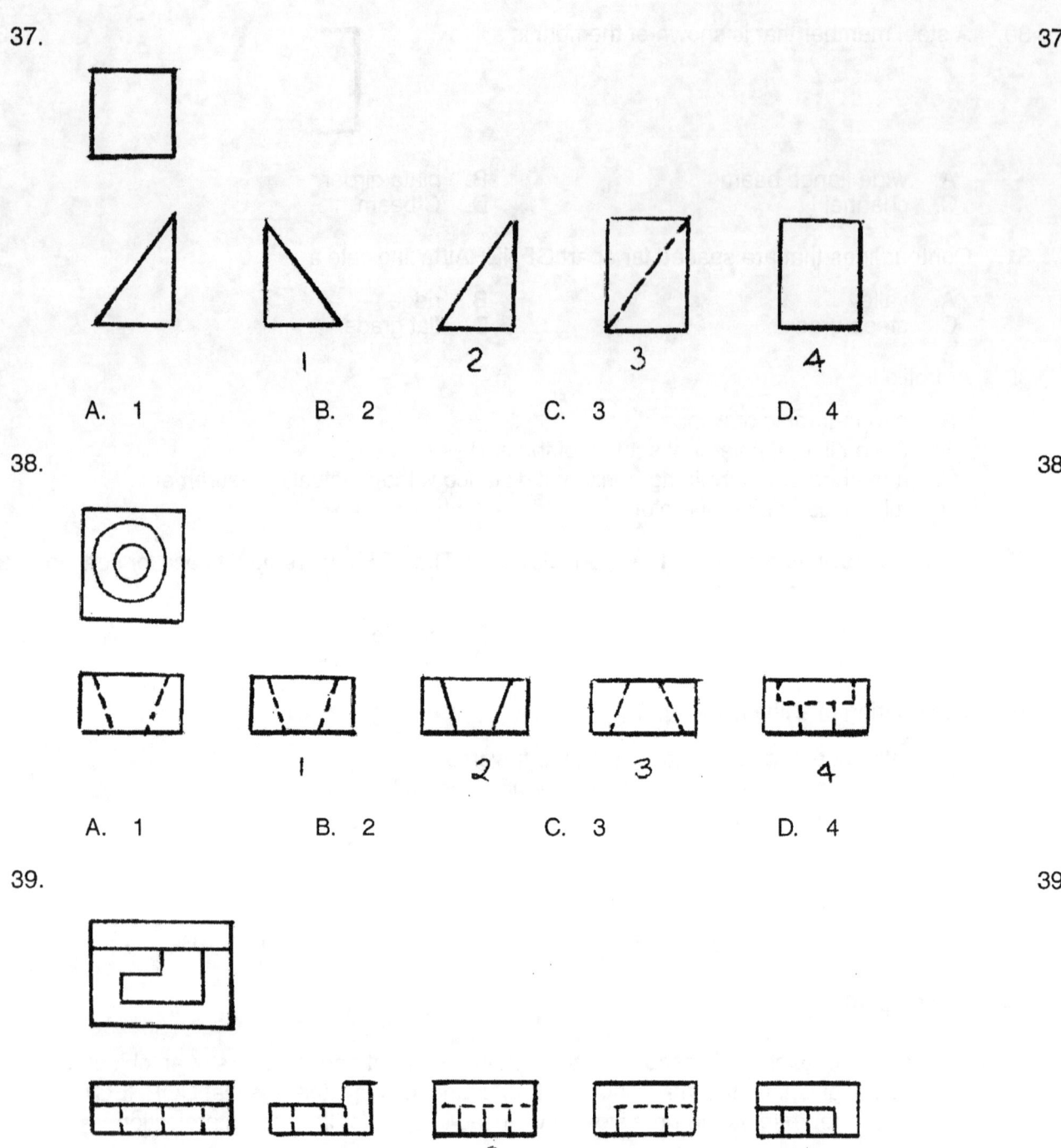

A. 1   B. 2   C. 3   D. 4

38.

A. 1   B. 2   C. 3   D. 4

39.

A. 1   B. 2   C. 3   D. 4

40.   40.____

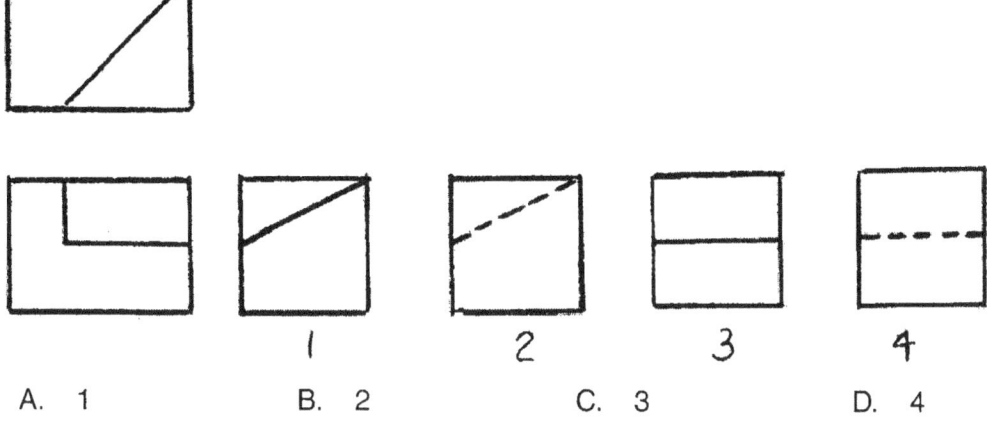

A. 1   B. 2   C. 3   D. 4

KEY (CORRECT ANSWERS)

1. C	11. B	21. C	31. D
2. C	12. D	22. B	32. B
3. D	13. B	23. C	33. D
4. B	14. C	24. A	34. B
5. C	15. C	25. A	35. A
6. B	16. C	26. C	36. B
7. D	17. D	27. D	37. D
8. D	18. A	28. A	38. A
9. A	19. D	29. C	39. A
10. B	20. B	30. C	40. C

EXAMINATION SECTION
TEST 1

DIRECTIONS: Each question or incomplete statement is followed by several suggested answers or completions. Select the one that BEST answers the question or completes the statement. *PRINT THE LETTER OF THE CORRECT ANSWER IN THE SPACE AT THE RIGHT.*

1. In leveling, a backsight on BM *A* is 4.270 and the foresight on TP #1 is 7.384. The elevation of BM *A* is 27.842.
   The HI is

   A. 17.399   B. 32.112   C. 39.213   D. 43.764

   1.____

2. A bill of materials calls for twenty-four 4" x 10" x 16'0" wooden beams.
   The number of FBM in these beams is

   A. 1210   B. 1230   C. 1250   D. 1280

   2.____

3. Two kinds of concrete are being used in the construction of a reinforced concrete building. Slump tests show one concrete to have a slump of 7 inches, the other 3 inches. The concrete with the 7 inch slump would be used for

   A. beams   B. floors   C. roof   D. columns

   3.____

4. A planimeter is used to

   A. measure the area of plane figures
   B. draw parallel lines
   C. measure the distance between parallel lines
   D. measure distances on plans

   4.____

5. The bearing of line AB is N65°W, that of line AC is S15°E.
   The angle BAC is

   A. 130°   B. 120°   C. 75°   D. 45°

   5.____

6. In a right triangle, the hypotenuse, AB, is 13 feet long. The side AC is 12 feet and side BC is 5 feet long. A perpendicular is dropped from C to side AB.
   Its length, in feet, in MOST NEARLY

   A. 4.4   B. 4.6   C. 4.9   D. 5.1

   6.____

7. The roots of the equation $2x^2 - x - 15 = 0$ are

   A. -3.0, +2.5   B. +3.0, -5.0
   C. +1.5, -5.0   D. +3.0, -2.5

   7.____

8. In laying out a horizontal circular curve for a highway,

   A. the center of the curve must be located on the ground
   B. full stations are located by deflection angles and chord distances
   C. field taping must be done along the arc of the curve
   D. an Engineer's Level must be used

   8.____

2 (#1)

9. In reinforced concrete construction, the reinforcing bars should be

   A. oiled to prevent rusting
   B. bent while at a red heat
   C. securely fastened so that they will not be displaced during the pour
   D. placed immediately after the concrete is poured

10. The distance between the zero and 100-foot marks of a steel tape is 99.9 feet. To lay out a true distance of 321.7 feet with this tape, the tape distance should be

    A. 319.7   B. 320.5   C. 322.0   D. 323.3

11.

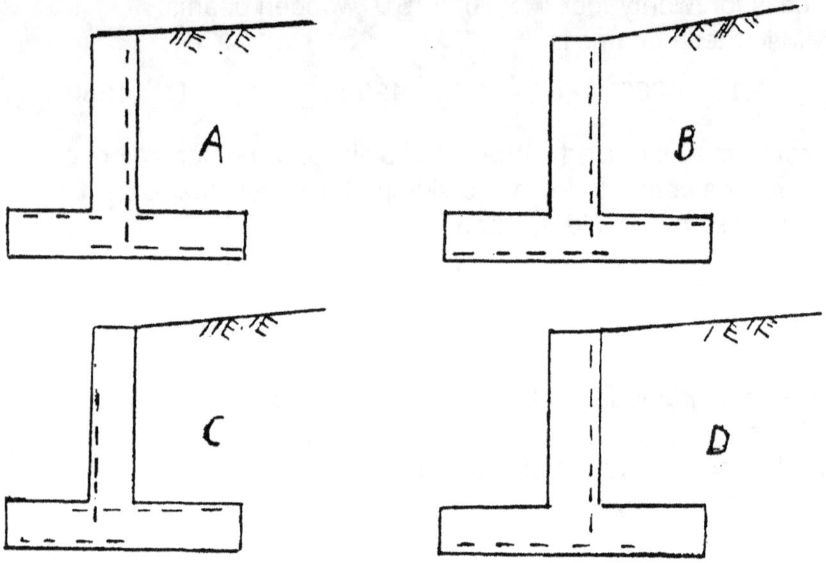

    In which one of the cantilever retaining walls shown above is the main reinforcing steel, indicated by the dotted lines, CORRECTLY located?

    A. A   B. B   C. C   D. D

12. The sensitivity of a bubble tube such as those on a transit or that on a level is a function of the

    A. length of the bubble tube
    B. spacing of the graduations on the tube
    C. radius of curvature of the inner surface of the glass forming the top of the tube
    D. length of the bubble within the bubble tube

13. The water pressure at a point 175 feet below the surface is, in pounds per square inch, MOST NEARLY

    A. 76   B. 79   C. 82   D. 85

14. The sum of the interior angles of a five-sided polygon is

    A. 390°   B. 480°   C. 540°   D. 660°

48

15. A true meridian on a map indicates 15.____

   A. true north
   B. the equator
   C. the latitude
   D. the direction of the magnetic pole

16. Points A, B, and C lie on the circumference of a circle with a 10-inch radius. Angle BAC is 45°. 16.____
   The length of chord BC is, in inches, MOST NEARLY

   A. 8.1   B. 9.1   C. 14.1   D. 15.1

17. The equations of two straight lines are y = 2x + 4 and y = 6 - x. 17.____
   They coordinate of the point of intersection is MOST NEARLY

   A. 5.31   B. 5.33   C. 5.35   D. 5.39

18. Which of the following statements with respect to contour lines is NOT correct? 18.____

   A. Contours crossing streams form vees which point upstream.
   B. A closed contour represents a hill or depression.
   C. Contours never cross except in the case of an overhanging cliff.
   D. The horizontal distance between contours does not vary with the slope of the ground.

19. A bill of material calls for 2 x 4's, S4S. The dressed size of this lumber is, in inches, 19.____

   A. 3 x 5   B. 1 5/8 x 3 7/8   C. 1 3/8 x 3 5/8   D. 1 5/8 x 3 5/8

20. Of the following terms, the one which is LEAST related to the others is 20.____

   A. azimuth   B. camber   C. batter   D. grade

21. The larger the Modulus of elasticity of a material, the 21.____

   A. *greater* the stress it can withstand
   B. *greater* the strain it can withstand
   C. *less* it will be strained for a given stress
   D. *less* it will be stressed for a given strain

22. In a simple reinforced concrete beam in a building, the concrete below the reinforcing steel serves PRIMARILY 22.____

   A. as fire protection
   B. to increase the shearing strength of the beam
   C. to simplify construction
   D. to prevent rusting of the steel

23. The foot-pound is a unit of 23.____

   A. power   B. work   C. force   D. capacity

24. The resistance of a 60 watt 110 volt light bulb is MOST NEARLY, in ohms, 24.____

   A. 60   B. 110   C. 160   D. 200

25. A horizontal force of 45 pounds is applied to a 60-pound weight which is suspended by a wire.
    When the system is in equilibrium, the tension in the wire is, in pounds,
    A. 75   B. 80   C. 85   D. 90

25.____

KEY (CORRECT ANSWERS)

1. B
2. D
3. D
4. A
5. A

6. B
7. D
8. B
9. C
10. C

11. B
12. C
13. A
14. C
15. A

16. C
17. B
18. D
19. D
20. A

21. C
22. A
23. B
24. D
25. A

SOLUTIONS TO PROBLEMS

1. **ANSWER: B**
   The HI is independent of the foresight measurement.
   HI = 27.842 + 4.270 = 32.112

2. **ANSWER: D**
   One board ft. = 144 in.

   NO. of FBM = $\dfrac{(16 \times 12)(4)(10)(24)}{144}$ =1280

5. **ANSWER: A**
   ∠BAC = (90 - 65) + 90 + 15
          = 130

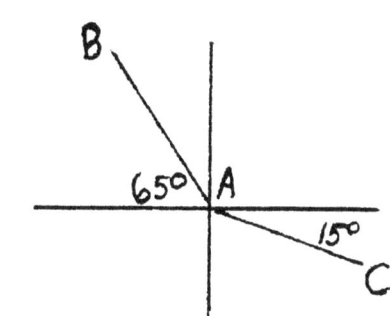

6. **ANSWER: B**
   sin B = 12/13 = y/5
   y = 60/13 = 4.6

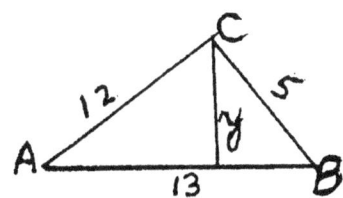

7. **ANSWER: D**
   (2x+5)(x-3) = 0
   x = -2.5; x = +3.0

10. **ANSWER: C**
    Error = 100 - 99.9 = 0.1 ft./100 ft. of true length
    ∴ 321.7 + 3(0.1) = 322.0 ft.

13. **ANSWER: A**
    One atmosphere (14.7 psi) = 34 ft. of water
    175/34 = 5.15 atm.
    (5.15)(14.7) = 76 psi.
    (This neglects the 1 atm. above the water surface.)

14. **ANSWER: C**
    For an n-sided polygon, the sum of the interior angles, say 2 a (for a regular polygon), is 2 an.
    2a = 180 - 360/n
    2na = 180n - 360 = 900 - 360 = 540° (for n=5)

16. ANSWER: C
    $AB^2 = BC^2 + CA^2$
    $BC = CA$
    $2CB^2 = AB^2 = (20)^2 - 400"$
    $CB^2 = 400/2 = 200"$
    $CB = \sqrt{200} = 10\sqrt{2}$
    CB 14,14"

    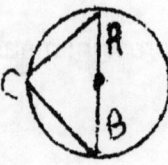

17. ANSWER: B
    $2x+4=6-x$; $x = 2/3$ at intersection
    $y = 2(2/3) + 4 = 5.33$

19. ANSWER: D
    According to American Lumber Standards, trimming of 2 x 4's to S4S means a 3/8 in. loss for each dimension.

21. ANSWER: C
    Modulus of elasticity = stress/strain. For a given stress, the strain decreases as the modulus increases.

23. ANSWER: B
    In general, work is force x distance.

24. ANSWER: D
    $P = VI = I^2R$
    $I = 60/110$; $R = V/I = (110)^2/60 \sim 200$

25. ANSWER: A
    The wire supports all the weight:
    T=75

    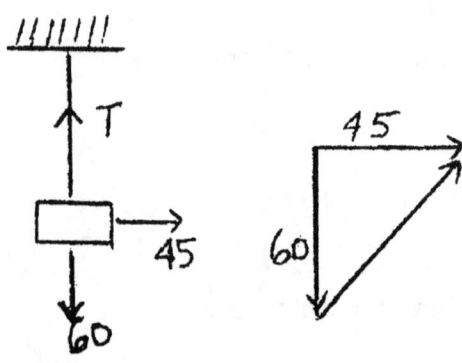

TEST 2

DIRECTIONS: Each question or incomplete statement is followed by several suggested answers or completions. Select the one that BEST answers the question or completes the statement. *PRINT THE LETTER OF THE CORRECT ANSWER IN THE SPACE AT THE RIGHT.*

1. A motor can raise a 3000-pound drop hammer with a velocity of 6 feet per second. Ignoring friction, the horsepower of the motor is

    A. 31.9 B. 32.7 C. 33.1 D. 34.3

2. In the system of pulleys shown at the right, the force F required to lift the 500 pound weight, ignoring friction, is MOST NEARLY.
    A. 990
    B. 450
    C. 250
    D. 100

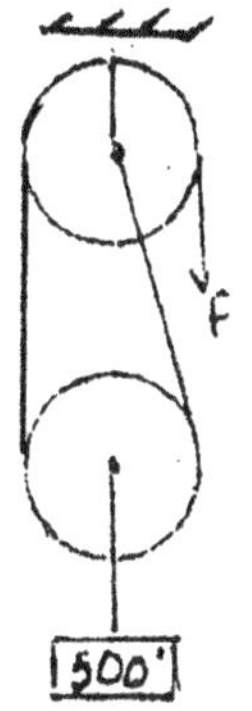

3. A flask weighing 225 grams when empty weighs 446 grams when filled with water and 419 grams when filled with oil. The specific gravity of the oil is about

    A. 0.88 B. 0.91 C. 0.93 D. 0.95

4. Piles are NOT driven by

    A. steam hammer   B. drop hammer
    C. jack   D. water hammer

5. A protractor is used to

    A. measure area
    B. draw parallel lines
    C. draw guidelines for lettering
    D. measure or layout angles on a scale drawing

6. Partial payments totaling $987,500 have been made on a contract of $1,750,000. The percentage of the TOTAL cost paid is

    A. 56.5 B. 57.2 C. 57.8 D. 58.2

7. Fire stopping PRIMARILY involves

    A. the placing of incombustible material over surfaces of combustible material
    B. replacing combustible with incombustible material
    C. the use of sprinklers and other protective devices
    D. the subdivision of large dead-air spaces

8. The MOST highly stressed rivet in in the gusset plate shown at the right is
   A. A
   B. B
   C. C
   D. D

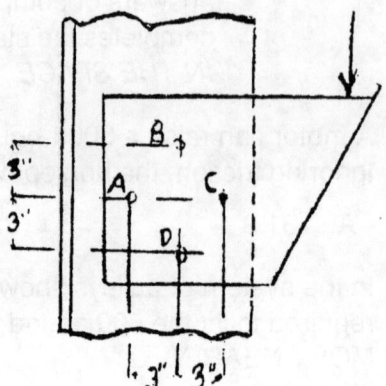

9. The built-in beam shown at the right will bend under load as shown in
   A. A
   B. B
   C. C
   D. D

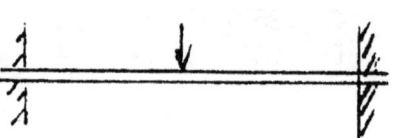

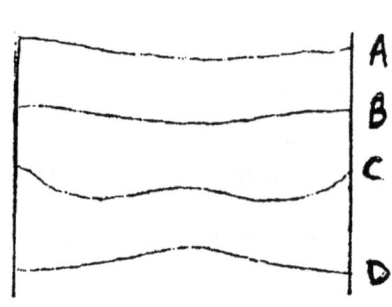

10. A vernier is a device used to
    A. measure fractional parts of a scale division
    B. measure the flow of water
    C. measure fluid pressure
    D. magnify objects

11. Of the following, the BEST pencil to use in taking field notes for a survey is
    A. H   B. 3H   C. 6H   D. 9H

12. A square is inscribed in a circle with a ten-inch diameter. The area of the square, in square inches, is
    A. 52   B. 51   C. 50   D. 49

13. A rectangular box is 10" long, 6" wide, and 4" high. The length of a diagonal drawn from the upper left rear corner to the lower right front corner is, in inches, MOST NEARLY
    A. 12.3   B. 12.4   C. 12.6   D. 12.8

14. A cam is USUALLY a _____ piece.
    A. circular, rotating   B. circular, non-rotating
    C. non-circular, rotating   D. non-circular, non-rotating

15. A right circular cone is 12 inches high, and the diameter of the base is 10 inches. The surface area of the cone is, in square inches, MOST NEARLY

 A. 196 B. 204 C. 210 D. 214

15.____

16. Of the following terms, the one which is LEAST related to the others is

 A. spindle B. key C. bolt D. rivet

16.____

Questions 17-20.

DIRECTIONS: Each of Questions 17 through 20 is related to one of the lettered items below. Mark the letter of the related item in the space at the right.

17. Sub punch

 A. mortar joint B. bridging
 C. roofing D. ream

17.____

18. Flashing

 A. mortar joint B. bridging
 C. roofing D. ream

18.____

19. Joist

 A. mortar joint B. bridging
 C. roofing D. ream

19.____

20. Point

 A. mortar joint B. bridging
 C. roofing D. ream

20.____

21. Of the following terms, the one which is LEAST related to the others is

 A. bevel B. pitch
 C. gage D. edge distance

21.____

22. In differential leveling, the following shots were taken from a single set-up: on T.P.#1, 5.643; on T.P.#2, 8.159. T.P.#1 is _____ than T.P.#2 by _____.

 A. *higher;* 13.802 B. *lower;* 13.802
 C. *higher;* 2.516 D. *lower;* 2.516

22.____

23. Of the following terms, the one which is LEAST related to the others is

 A. course B. stud C. bat D. bond

23.____

24.
A.
B.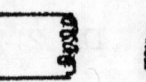
C.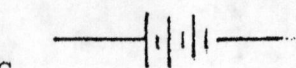
D.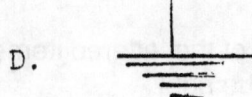

In the symbols shown above, the one which represents a battery is

A. A   B. B   C. C   D. D

25. A 6" diameter steel pipe, 100 feet long, installed at 60° F conveys steam at 220° F. If the coefficient of linear expansion is 0.0000065 per degree Fahrenheit, the number of feet that the pipe expands is MOST NEARLY

A. .098   B. .104   C. .108   D. .116

KEY (CORRECT ANSWERS)

1. B   11. B
2. C   12. C
3. A   13. A
4. D   14. C
5. D   15. B

6. A   16. A
7. D   17. D
8. C   18. C
9. B   19. B
10. A   20. A

21. A
22. C
23. B
24. C
25. B

SOLUTIONS TO PROBLEMS

1. ANSWER: B
   Power = (3000)(6) = 18,000 ft-lb/sec.
   One HP = 550 ft-lb/sec.
   P = 18,000/550 = 32.7 HP

2. ANSWER: C
   Mechanical advantage = 2
   2F = 500; F = 250

3. ANSWER: A
   Wt. of water = 446 - 225 = 221
   Wt. of oil = 419 - 225 = 194
   Sp. gr. = 194/221 = 0.875

6. ANSWER: A

   $$\frac{9.875 \times 10^5}{1.75 \times 10^5} \times 10^2 = 56.5\%$$

12. ANSWER: C
    Diagonal of square = x/2

    Then $10 = x\sqrt{2}$

    $x = 10\sqrt{2}$

    Field of square = x^2

    $x^2 = (10/\sqrt{2})^2 = 100/2 = 50$

    OR

    A(field of square) = x^2 and
    $x^2 = 5^2 + 5^2 - 50$

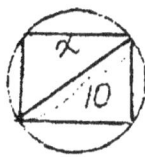

13. ANSWER: A
    $y^2 = 10^2 + 6^2 = 136"$
    $x^2 = y^2 + 4^2 = 152"$
    $x = \sqrt{152} = 12.33"$ (most nearly)

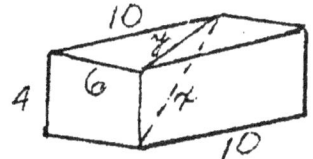

15. ANSWER: B

    The curved surface of a right circular cone is $\pi r \sqrt{r^2 + h^2}$

    A = $(\pi)(5)\sqrt{25+144} = 65\pi \sim 204$ (does not include area of the base)

22. ANSWER: C
    The larger number read on the scale refers to the lower level: 8.159 - 5.643 = 2.516

25. ANSWER: B
    Expansion = (100 ft.)(220 - 60°)(6.5 x 10^{-6}) - 0.104 ft.

TEST 3

DIRECTIONS: Each question or incomplete statement is followed by several suggested answers or completions. Select the one that BEST answers the question or completes the statement. *PRINT THE LETTER OF THE CORRECT ANSWER IN THE SPACE AT THE RIGHT.*

1. Of the symbols shown above for materials in section, the one representing glass is

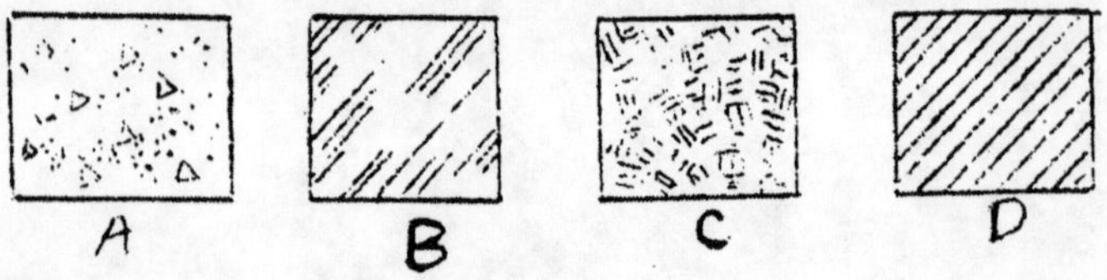

    A. A   B. B   C. C   D. D

    1.____

2. Of the symbols shown in the question above, for materials in section, the one representing cast iron is

    A. A   B. B   C. C   D. D

    2.____

Questions 3-6.

DIRECTIONS: Each of Questions 3 through 6 is related but in an opposite sense to one of the items marked A, B, C, and D. As an example, the terms *longitudinal* and *transverse* are related in that they both refer to direction, but, of course, the directions are at right angles. Indicate in the space at the right the OPPOSITE to the terms in these questions.

3. Tap

    A. Mantissa   B. Departure   C. Spiget   D. Die

    3.____

4. Bell

    A. Mantissa   B. Departure   C. Spiget   D. Die

    4.____

5. Latitude

    A. Mantissa   B. Departure   C. Spiget   D. Die

    5.____

6. Characteristic

    A. Mantissa   B. Departure   C. Spiget   D. Die

    6.____

Questions 7-11.

DIRECTIONS: In each of the following groups of drawings, the top view and front elevation of an object are shown at the left. At the right are four drawings, one of which represents the end elevation of the object as seen from the right. Select the drawing which represents the CORRECT end elevation.

NOTE: The first group is shown as a sample only. Which drawing represents the CORRECT end elevation?

A. A   B. B   C. C   D. D

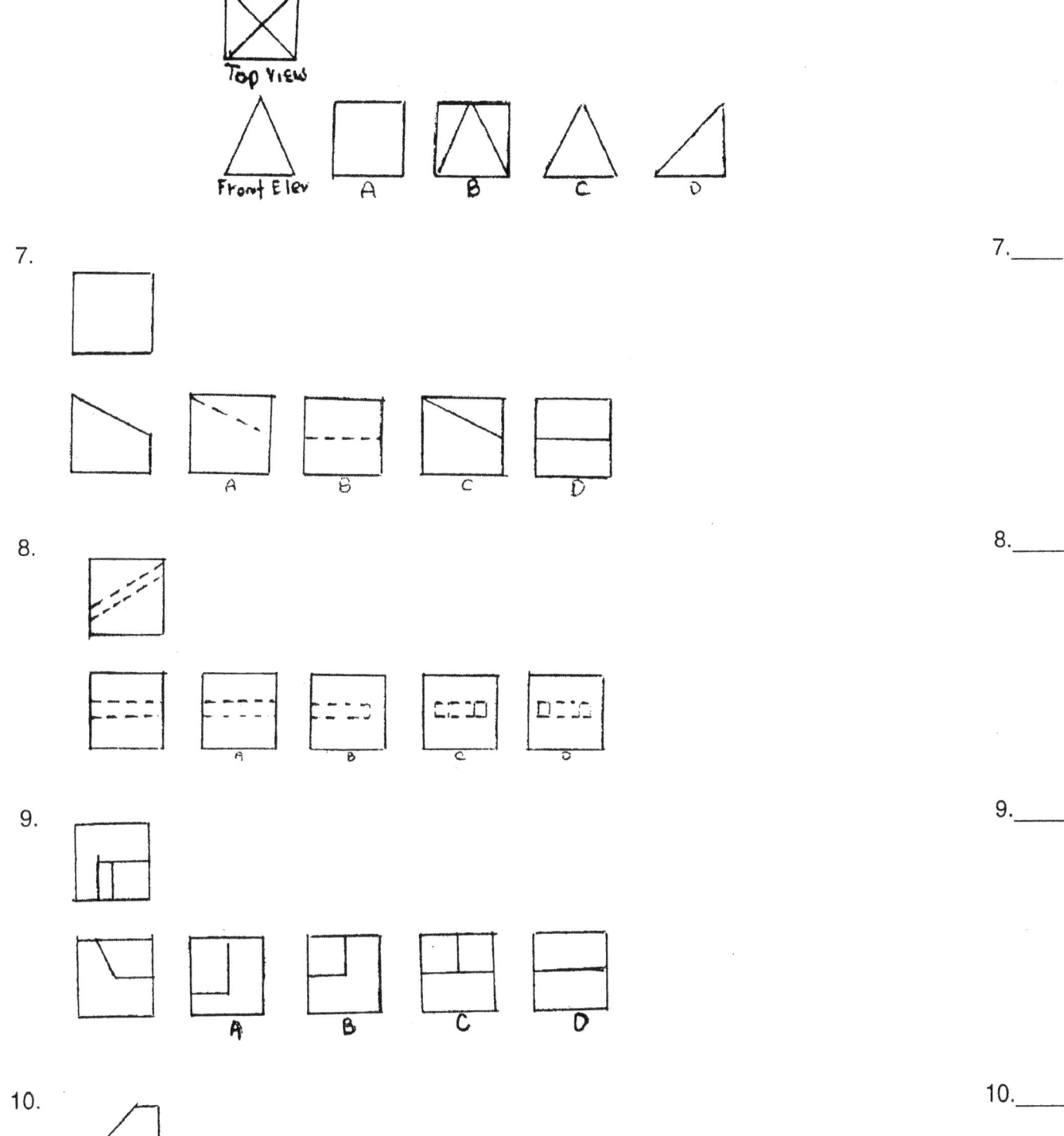

11.

[Figure: top view of a square pyramid, with four options A, B, C, D showing different unfolded/developed views]

12. Ten-penny nails

    A. are 10 inches long
    B. cost 10 cents per dozen
    C. weigh 10 pounds per thousand
    D. are not a commercial size

13. A dimension on a blueprint marked 3'4" is scaled and found to be 1 1/4". A second dimension on the same print scales 2 7/16".
    The second dimension should be marked

    A. 6'3"   B. 6'6"   C. 6'8"   D. 6'9"

14. The logarithm of 2 is 0.30103. The logarithm of 0.25 is

    A. 9.39689-10   B. 9.39791-10
    C. 9.39793-10   D. 9.39796-10

15. A 1:2:3 1/2 concrete has a water-cement ratio of 6 gallons per sack of cement.
    The strength of the concrete can be increased by decreasing the

    A. ratio of the fine aggregate to cement
    B. ratio of the coarse aggregate to cement
    C. ratio of both fine and coarse aggregate to cement
    D. water-cement ratio

16. A spiral easement curve is NOT used

    A. to connect a tangent and a circular curve
    B. to connect two circular curves of different radii
    C. to connect two tangents
    D. at any time in highway work

17. Batter boards are used to

    A. define construction lines on the ground
    B. prevent splatter of concrete when pouring
    C. absorb shock in construction work
    D. barricade the construction area

18. In surveying, *double hubbing* or *double reversing* is done with a

    A. transit   B. level   C. tape   D. alidado

19. The inner surfaces of forms for concrete are oiled

    A. to prevent rusting
    B. to make removal of forms easier
    C. to prevent honeycombing
    D. when a stiff concrete mixture is being used

20. Installation of a sprinkler system would be LEAST complicated when the type of building construction is

    A. flat slab   B. beam and girder
    C. steel frame   D. brick bearing wall

21. Of the following items, the one which is NOT an opening protective is fire

    A. door   B. tower   C. shutter   D. window

22. A load is to be supported by two 2 x 4's on a long simple span.
    The BEST way to arrange the 2 x 4's for maximum strength is

    A.

    B.

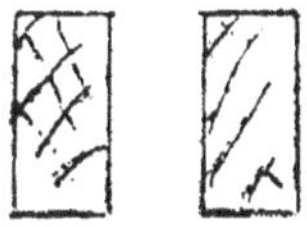

    C.

    D.

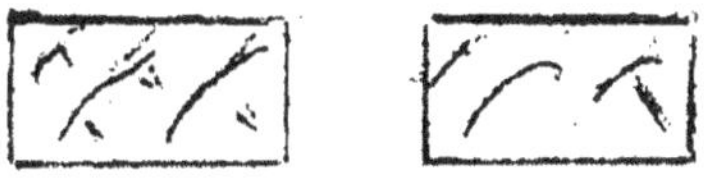

Questions 23-24.

   DIRECTIONS: Questions 23 and 24 are to be answered on the basis of the truss shown below.

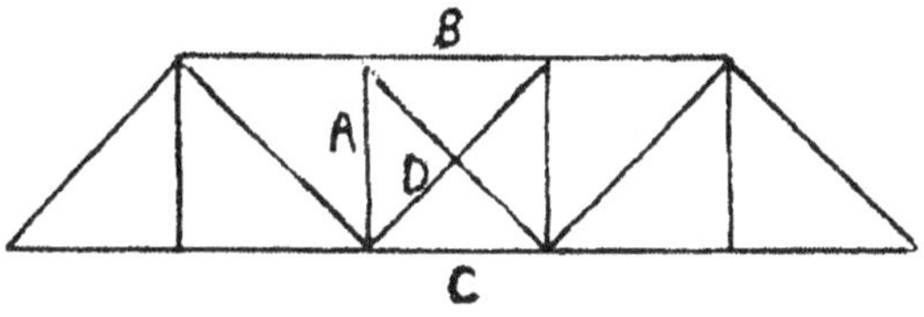

23. The compression chord member is marked

    A. A   B. B   C. C   D. D

24. The tension chord member is marked

    A. A   B. B   C. C   D. D

25. A small by-pass on a large gate valve serves PRIMARILY

    A. to reduce the unbalanced pressure on the gate when opening the valve
    B. as a by-pass in case the valve cannot be opened
    C. to meter the flow through the valve
    D. to tell which way the water is flowing

KEY (CORRECT ANSWERS)

1.	B	11.	A
2.	D	12.	C
3.	D	13.	B
4.	C	14.	C
5.	B	15.	D
6.	A	16.	C
7.	D	17.	A
8.	C	18.	A
9.	B	19.	B
10.	A	20.	A

21. B
22. A
23. B
24. C
25. A

SOLUTIONS TO PROBLEMS

7. ANSWER: D
   The perspective drawings are as follows:

   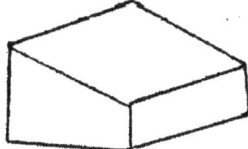

8. ANSWER: C

   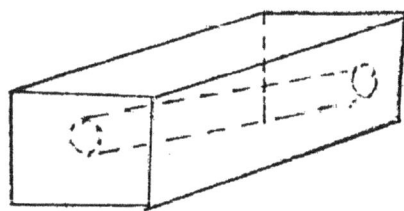

9. ANSWER: B

   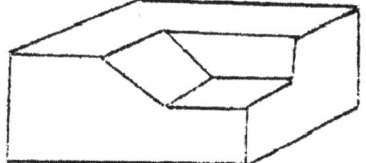

10. ANSWER: A

    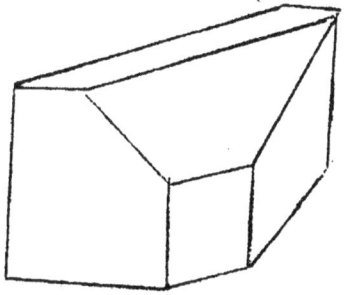

    (As seen from rear of front elevation)

11. ANSWER: A

    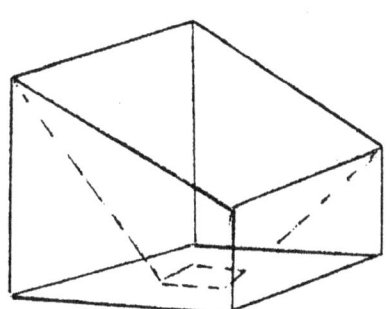

13. ANSWER: B
    Scale = 5/4 in. per 40 in. = 1/32 in./in.
    At a scale of 2 7/16 in., the second dimension is
    (39/16)(32) = 78 in. = 6'6"

14. ANSWER: C
    Log (1/4) = log 2^{-2} = (-2 x 0.30103) = 0.60206
    = 9.39794-10

TEST 4

DIRECTIONS: Each question or incomplete statement is followed by several suggested answers or completions. Select the one that BEST answers the question or completes the statement. *PRINT THE LETTER OF THE CORRECT ANSWER IN THE SPACE AT THE RIGHT.*

1. The joints of bell-and-spigot cast iron water mains are filled with   1._____

    A. lead   B. copper   C. rubber   D. oakum

2. Parallax exists in a transit when the   2._____

    A. line of sight is parallel to the long bubble
    B. cross-hairs appear to move over the object sighted when the observer's eye is moved slightly
    C. line of sight is perpendicular to the horizontal axis
    D. vertical axis is perpendicular to the horizontal axis

3. In unlined tunnel work, survey points are USUALLY located on   3._____

    A. the roof   B. the walls
    C. the floor   D. suspended platforms

4. The grit chamber of a sewage plant removes heavy solids such as sand by   4._____

    A. allowing the sewage to flow over a weir
    B. reducing the velocity of flow
    C. stopping the flow completely
    D. screens

5. Small sewer pipe is USUALLY made of   5._____

    A. cast iron, cement lined   B. steel
    C. concrete   D. vitrified clay

6. A timber weighing 500 pounds is to be dragged over a stone floor with a rope which makes an angle of 45 with the horizontal.   6._____
If the coefficient of static friction is 0.4, the tension in the rope necessary to start the timber moving is, in pounds, MOST NEARLY

    A. 196   B. 202   C. 208   D. 214

7. A stadia survey would MOST probably be made in connection with   7._____

    A. a building layout
    B. a topographic map
    C. the location of bridge piers
    D. the erection of steel

8. The flanges and web of an H-section 12" wide by 12" deep are one inch thick. Steel weighs 490 pounds per cubic foot.   8._____
A 10'0" length of this column would weigh, in pounds, MOST NEARLY

    A. 1150   B. 1250   C. 1350   D. 1450

9. The term *bond,* as used in connection with brick work, refers to the

   A. adhesion of mortar to brick
   B. metal anchors used to tie beams to wall
   C. arrangement of the bricks within the wall
   D. ties used to hold the brick to the backing

10. [Sketch: loads of 10,000, 20,000, 20,000 with spacings 8'0" and 12'0"]

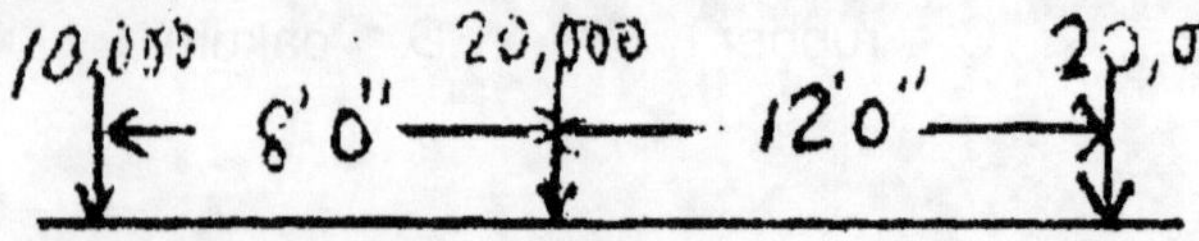

    The center of gravity of the three concentrated loads shown in the sketch above is located a distance, in feet, from the right load of

    A. 8.4   B. 8.6   C. 8.8   D. 9.0

11. A Philadelphia Rod which can be used with or without a target

    A. is a sighting pole used for line work
    B. has a movable ribbon
    C. has a pointed shoe
    D. has graduations 0.01 feet wide

12. An airplane is flying at 240 mph (air speed). A wind of 100 mph is blowing at right angles to the longitudinal axis of the plane.
    The ground speed of the airplane is, in mph,

    A. 220   B. 240   C. 260   D. 280

Questions 13-17.

DIRECTIONS: Each of Questions 13 through 17 is related to one of the lettered items below. Indicate the CORRECT answer.

13. Fillet

A. buck	B. cable	C. parapet
D. bond	E. weld	F. plaster

14. Coping

A. buck	B. cable	C. parapet
D. bond	E. weld	F. plaster

15. Jamb

A. buck	B. cable	C. parapet
D. bond	E. weld	F. plaster

16. Stretcher

A. buck	B. cable	C. parapet
D. bond	E. weld	F. plaster

17. Bx

A. buck	B. cable	C. parapet
D. bond	E. weld	F. plaster

18. A block of wood of specific gravity 0.6 weighs 10 pounds. Its volume, in cubic feet, is MOST NEARLY

   A. .027   B. 0.27   C. 2.7   D. 27

19. A rectangular barge weighs 1,000,000 pounds when fully loaded and has outside dimensions of 60 feet long, 30 feet wide, and 10 feet deep.
    In fresh water, it sinks to a depth, in feet, MOST NEARLY of

   A. 7.7   B. 7.9   C. 8.9   D. 9.9

20. A gas in a compressor cylinder under an absolute pressure of 14.7 pounds per square inch has a volume of 6 cubic inches. It is compressed so slowly that its temperature does not vary, to a pressure of 100 pounds per square inch absolute.
    Its volume now is, in cubic inches, MOST NEARLY

   A. 0.58   B. 0.68   C. 0.78   D. 0.88

21. A quantity of mercury is heated, and Fahrenheit and Centigrade thermometers are immersed in it. The reading on the Fahrenheit scale is exactly twice the reading on the centigrade scale.
    The reading on the Fahrenheit scale is

   A. 320   B. 360   C. 400   D. 440

22. A piece of metal 6 inches in diameter is being turned in a lathe.
    If the recommended cutting speed is 500 feet per minute, the required revolutions per minute of the spindle is MOST NEARLY

   A. 320   B. 2130   C. 1320   D. 120

23. A building is being raised by a jack preparatory to underpinning the structure. The load on the jack is 4000 pounds. The jack screw has a pitch of 2 threads per inch.
    Ignoring friction, the force, in pounds, applied at a point on a capstan bar 3'0" from the axis of the jack screw required to raise the building is MOST NEARLY

   A. 288   B. 144   C. 72   D. 9

24. Of the following items, the one that is LEAST related to the others in function is

   A. bulldozer   B. clamshell
   C. backhoe   D. A-frame

25. One pound of lead at 200° F is placed in one pound of water which is at a temperature of 60° F. In a short time, both attain the same temperature of 64.3.
    The specific heat of lead as determined above, in BTU per pound per degree Fahrenheit, is MOST NEARLY

   A. .0137   B. .0217   C. .0317   D. .0537

KEY (CORRECT ANSWERS)

1.	A	11.	D
2.	B	12.	C
3.	A	13.	E
4.	B	14.	C
5.	D	15.	A
6.	B	16.	D
7.	B	17.	B
8.	A	18.	B
9.	C	19.	C
10.	C	20.	D

21. A
22. A
23. D
24. D
25. C

SOLUTIONS TO PROBLEMS

6. ANSWER: B
   F = kN, where N = normal force between the surfaces, and
   k = coefficient of static friction
   ∴ F min. = (500)(0.4) = 200

   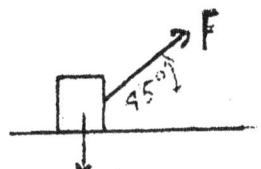

8. ANSWER: A
   Two sections have volume,
   V_1 = (10)(1)(1/12).
   One section has V_2 = (10/12)(1/12)(10)
   Weight = $(2V_1 + V_2)(490)$ ~ 1150

   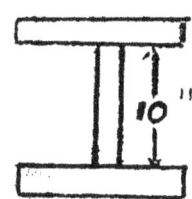

10. ANSWER: C
    50,000x = (20,000)(12)+(10,000)(20)   x = 8.8

    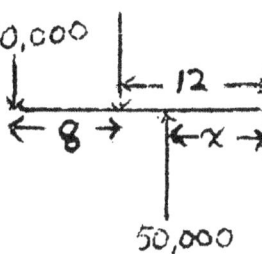

12. ANSWER: C
    $V = \sqrt{100^2 + 200^2} = 260$

    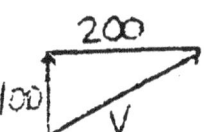

18. ANSWER: B
    Density = (0.6)(62.4) lb./ft.^{3}
    Volume = 10/(0.6)(62.4) ~ 0.27

19. ANSWER: C
    10^6 lbs. will displace 106/62.4 = 1.6 x 10^4 ft.^{3} of water.
    Since cross section = 60 x 30 ft.^{2}, depth = 1.6 x 10^4/60 x30 = 8.9 ft.

20. ANSWER: D
    Boyle's law: PV = constant
    (14.7)(6)   = (100 x V)
            V = 0.882 ft.^{3}

21. ANSWER: A
    In general, °F. = (9/5)°C + 32
    When F = 2C,
    ∴   F = (9/5)(F/2) + 32
        F = 320°

22. **ANSWER: A**

   The initial circumference of the piece is $\pi D = \pi/2$ ft.

   $\therefore 500/(\pi/2) = 320$ ft. per min.

23. **ANSWER: D**

   The mechanical advantage of a screw or jack =

   $2\pi l/p$ (l = length of force arm, p = pitch of the screw)

   Mech. Adv. = $(2\pi)(36)/0.5 = 144\pi$.

   Force = $4000/144\pi \sim 9$ lb.

24. **ANSWER: C**

   $Q = m\, C_p\, \Delta t$

   For water, $C_p = 1$ Btu/lb./°F.
   $(1.0)(1.0)(64.3 - 60) = (1.0)(C_p)(200 - 64.3)$
   $C_p = 4.3/135.7 = 0.0317$

EXAMINATION SECTION
TEST 1

DIRECTIONS: Each question or incomplete statement is followed by several suggested answers or completions. Select the one that BEST answers the question or completes the statement. *PRINT THE LETTER OF THE CORRECT ANSWER IN THE SPACE AT THE RIGHT.*

1. 0.8021 feet is, in inches, MOST NEARLY

    A. 9 1/4 B. 9 3/8 C. 9 1/2 D. 9 5/8

2. The structural steel shape MOST often used as a stair stringer is a

    A. channel B. angle C. tee D. zee

3. The abbreviation M.S.L. appearing on a topographic map means

    A. measure straight lengths
    B. make side longer
    C. mean sea level
    D. most safe lintel

4. A specification for sand to be used in concrete requires that sand be well graded. *Well graded* means that the particles be

    A. minute
    B. coarse
    C. of variable sizes
    D. of one size

5. A vertical transverse profile in a street showing the underground utilities is called a(n) _____-section.

    A. cross B. contour C. invert D. front

6. The seepage of ground water into a sewer line is known as

    A. ingestion
    B. infiltration
    C. attrition
    D. dilution

7. The number of board feet in 15 pieces of 2' x 6" x 12' feet of lumber is

    A. 180 B. 360 C. 1080 D. 2160

8. The diameter of pipe, in inches, required to carry a flow of 1200 G.P.M. at a velocity of 4.91 f.p.s. is MOST NEARLY (7.48 gal. =1 cu.ft.)

    A. 8 B. 10 C. 12 D. 14

9. If the thickness of the steel wall of a 24 inch diameter water main is 1/2 inch and the water pressure in the water main is 125 p.s.i., then the unit stress in the steel, in p.s.i., is MOST NEARLY

    A. 1500 B. 2000 C. 2500 D. 3000

10. An interior angle of a five-sided traverse is measured six times and recorded as 250°55'30".
    The angle is MOST NEARLY

    A. 40°12'30" B. 40°18'5" C. 41°19'15" D. 41°49'15"

11. The total number of square feet of floor area in three rooms whose measurements are 12'8" x 10'0", 10'2" x 11'8", and 12'5" x 13'8", respectively, is MOST NEARLY

    A. 410   B. 415   C. 420   D. 425

Questions 12-13.

DIRECTIONS: Questions 12 and 13 refer to the following surveying leveling notes.

STA	BS	HI	FS	ELEV
BM_1	6.23'			84.47'
TP_1	5.67'		8.29'	
TP_2	7.48'		3.41'	
BM_2			4.53'	

12. The HI of BM_1 is, in feet,

    A. 77.24   B. 79.36   C. 87.58   D. 89.70

13. The ELEV TP_2 is, in feet,

    A. 82.59   B. 83.67   C. 85.70   D. 87.18

14. A #6 bar has an area equivalent to a circle whose diameter is

    A. 1/4"   B. 1/2"   C. 3/4"   D. 1"

15.
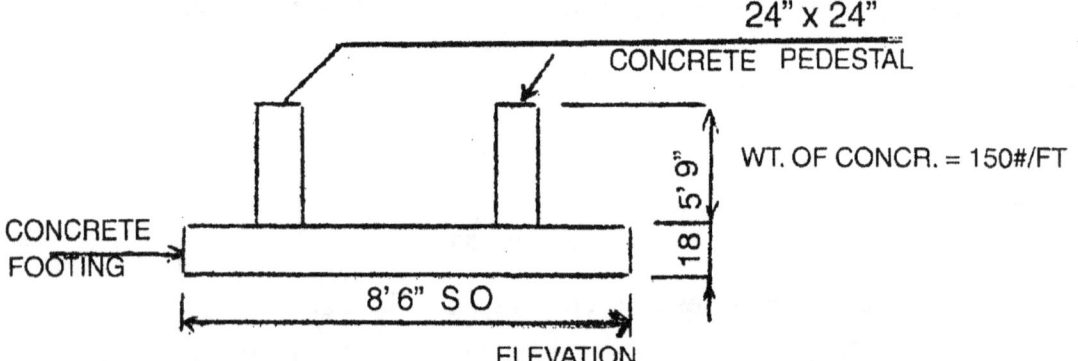
ELEVATION

The total weight, in pounds, of the above concrete footing and pedestal is MOST NEARLY

    A. 20,200   B. 23,100   C. 32,600   D. 41,500

16. The capacity, in gallons, of a flat head steel tank 38 inches in diameter by five feet long is MOST NEARLY (7.5 gal. = 1 cu.ft.)

    A. 250   B. 275   C. 295   D. 315

17. The drafting symbol ——⊳⊲—— on a piping drawing indicates a _____ valve.

    A. globe
    C. check
    B. butterfly
    D. pressure relief

18. If the floor to floor height in a building is 9'6" and there are 15 equal risers, then the height of each riser is, in inches, MOST NEARLY

    A. 7.3   B. 7.4   C. 7.5   D. 7.6

19. A 2,200 feet long pipeline, 18 I.D., carries water at 5.06 feet per second. If the f is 0.02, then the total loss in head due to friction in the pipeline, in feet of water, is MOST NEARLY (hf = flv²/d2g)

    A. 9.4   B. 10.5   C. 11.6   D. 12.3

20.

    The cross bracing labeled X on the ELEVATION shown above is called

    A. bridging   B. studding   C. shimming   D. joisting

21.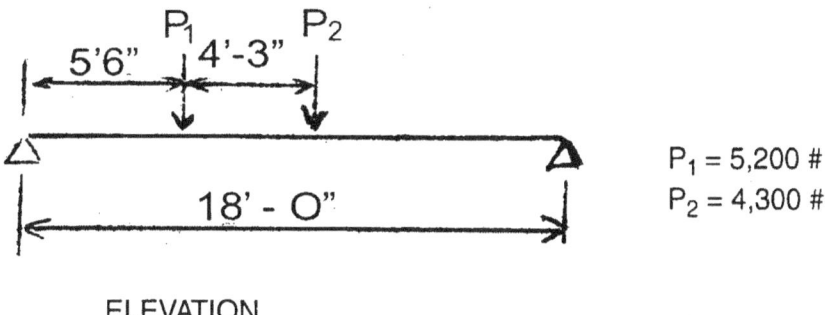

    $P_1 = 5,200$ #
    $P_2 = 4,300$ #

    ELEVATION

    The vertical shear, in pounds, one foot to the right of the concentrated load P_1, in the ELEVATION shown above, is MOST NEARLY

    A. 380   B. 520   C. 750   D. 930

22.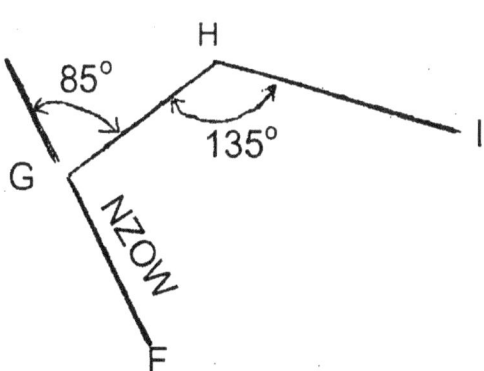

    In the layout shown on the preceding page, the bearing of line HI is

    A. N70E   B. N10W   C. S70E   D. N70W

23. A stairway with 7 treads needs _____ risers.

    A. 6   B. 7   C. 8   D. 9

24.

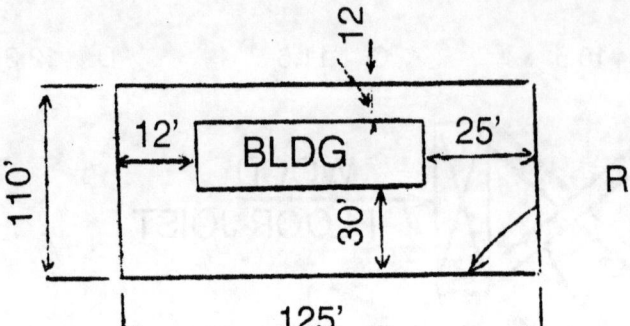

PLOT PLAN

In the above shown plot plan, the number of cubic yards of top soil, 6" deep, required to cover the tract is MOST NEARLY

    A. 115   B. 125   C. 135   D. 145

25. In structural steel work, it is usual practice NOT to paint surfaces that have been

    A. burned   B. sheared   C. milled   D. coped

KEY (CORRECT ANSWERS)

1. D		11. B	
2. A		12. D	
3. C		13. B	
4. C		14. C	
5. A		15. B	
6. B		16. C	
7. A		17. A	
8. B		18. D	
9. D		19. C	
10. D		20. A	

    21. A
    22. C
    23. C
    24. D
    25. C

TEST 2

DIRECTIONS: Each question or incomplete statement is followed by several suggested answers or completions. Select the one that BEST answers the question or completes the statement. *PRINT THE LETTER OF THE CORRECT ANSWER IN THE SPACE AT THE RIGHT.*

Questions 1-2.

DIRECTIONS: Questions 1 and 2 refer to the following sketch.

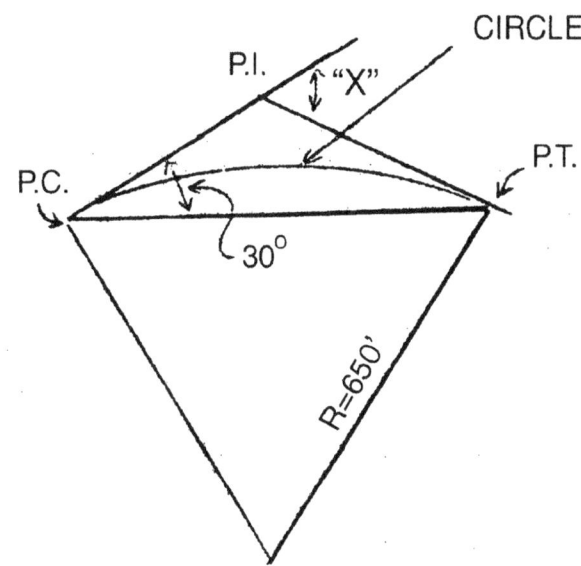

1. The angle X is

   A. 30° B. 40° C. 50° D. 60°

2. The chord distance P.C. to P.T. is _____ feet.

   A. 225 B. 330 C. 650 D. 725

3. The is equal to MOST NEARLY

   A. 13.85 B. 13.90 C. 13.95 D. 14.00

4. A sounding with a lead line shows that the depth in the river is 29.8 feet. If the sounding is taken when the tide gage reads +3.4 feet above M.S.L. and the local datum is 1.9' above M.S.L., then the elevation of the bottom of the river with respect to the local datum is, in feet, MOST NEARLY

   A. -26.4 B. -28.3 C. -31.7 D. -35.1

5. The shaded area expressed algebraically is
   A. $4(X+Y/2)X$
   B. $4(x^2+y^2)$
   C. $(x+y)(x-y)$
   D. $4(X+Y)X-2$

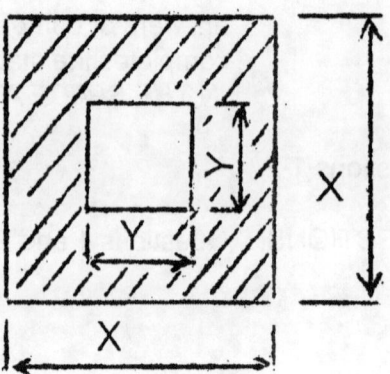

6. The valve that is placed before a fire hydrant in the city is a(n) _____ valve.
   A. angle   B. gate   C. check   D. globe

7. Of the following, the DENSEST liquid is
   A. oil   B. water   C. alcohol   D. mercury

8. The run-off, in C.F.S., from a tract 300 ft. x 830 ft., for a rainfall of 1.5 inches per hour and run-off 0.82 is MOST NEARLY (Q = C.i.A., when A is in acres. 1 acre = 43,560 sq.ft.)
   A. 4   B. 5   C. 6   D. 7

9. The resisting-moment, in foot kips, of the steel in a reinforced concrete beam whose A_s is 1.50, f_s is 24,000 p.s.i., j is 7/8, and effective depth 18 inches is MOST NEARLY ($M_s = A_s f_s j d$)
   A. 41   B. 43   C. 45   D. 47

10.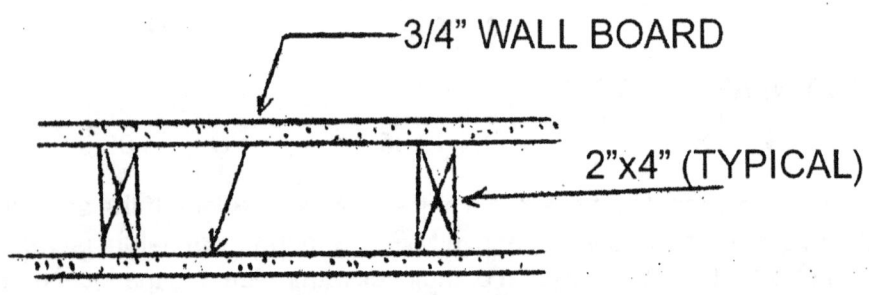

   PLAN - PARTITION WALL

   In the plan shown above, the 2" x 4" member is called a
   A. joist   B. stud   C. cove   D. sheath

11. In the city, reinforcing steel is bent and placed by
   A. ornamental iron workers
   B. miscellaneous iron workers
   C. carpenters
   D. metal lathers

12. The white encrustation on the face of a wall caused by the presence of salts in the mortar or bricks is called   12.____

    A. amberescence   B. deliquescense
    C. efflorescence   D. echinuscense

13. A dam can be built *without* diverting the river by using   13.____

    A. corewalls   B. cofferdams
    C. channels   D. wallpoints

14. Of the following pipe materials, the one that is MOST commonly used to convey drinking water is   14.____

    A. clay   B. wood
    C. cast iron   D. polyethylene plastic

15. A gooseneck is MOST often required on a(n)   15.____

    A. steam line   B. water service line
    C. sewer house connection   D. electric house service

16. The x----x----x----x appearing on a topographical map represents a _____ line.   16.____

    A. fence   B. bulkhead   C. subway   D. water

17. In the sketch shown at the right, the horizontal molded projection at the top of the building is a   17.____
    A. camber
    B. cornice
    C. coping
    D. cant

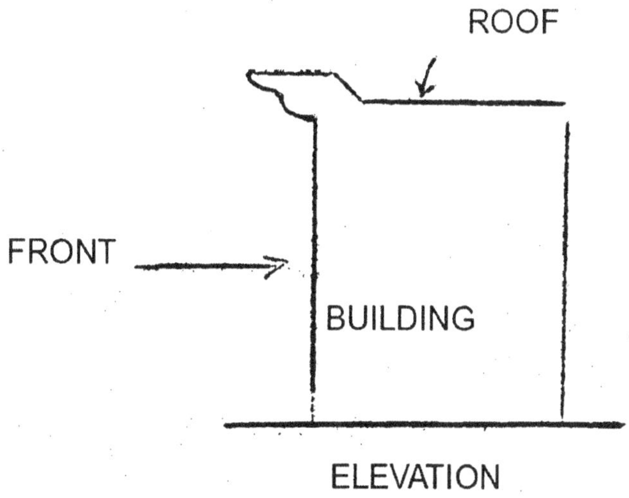

18. The moment of inertia, of the rectangle shown at the right, about the X-X axis is MOST NEARLY (I = 1/12bd^3)   18.____

    A. 162 ft^3
    B. 182.3 ft^3
    C. 364.5 ft^3
    D. 729 ft^3

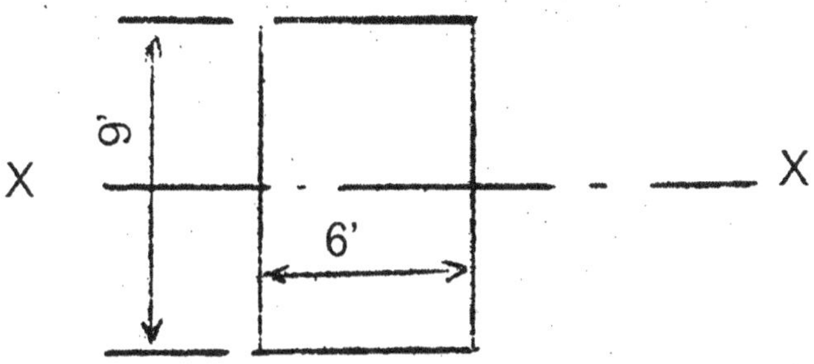

19. Galvanizing a steel surface USUALLY means coating it with   19.____

    A. cadmium   B. zinc   C. lead   D. tin

4 (#2)

20. Of the following elements, the one that is LEAST active chemically is   20._____

    A. copper   B. lead   C. zinc   D. iron

21. The hydraulic radius of a circular pipe flowing full is   21._____

    A. r/2   B. 2/r   C. r/1   D. 1/r

22. The position in which the weld shown at the right is being made is   22._____
    A. side
    B. vertical
    C. flat
    D. horizontal

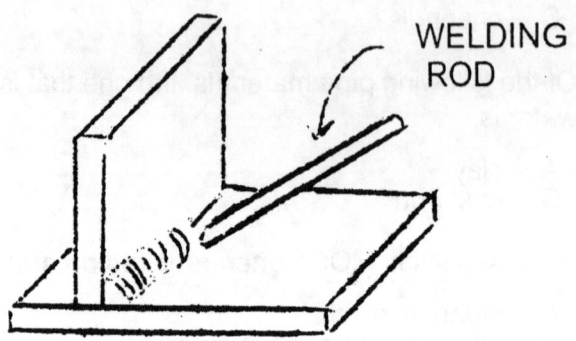

23. The figure shown at the right shows the results of a survey made with a 100.00 ft. steel tape. The tape was later standardized and found to be 99.97 feet long. The CORRECT perimeter, in feet, based on the true length of the tape is MOST NEARLY   23._____
    A. 2466.97
    B. 2467.04
    C. 2467.50
    D. 2468.57

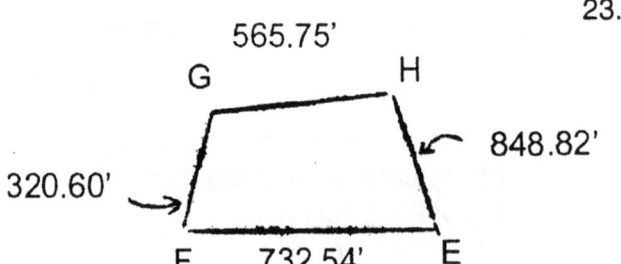

24. Of the following elements, the one that is PREDOMINANT in structural is   24._____

    A. S   B. F_e C. S_i D. M_n

25.   25._____

For the beam loading shown above, the shear diagram should look MOST NEARLY like

5 (#2)

A. B.

C. D.

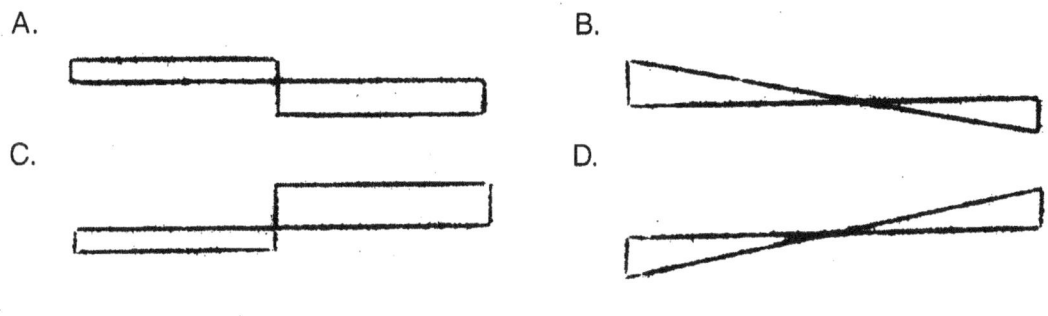

KEY (CORRECT ANSWERS)

1.	D	11.	D
2.	C	12.	C
3.	B	13.	B
4.	B	14.	C
5.	C	15.	B
6.	B	16.	A
7.	D	17.	B
8.	D	18.	C
9.	D	19.	B
10.	B	20.	B

21. A
22. D
23. A
24. B
25. A

TEST 3

DIRECTIONS: Each question or incomplete statement is followed by several suggested answers or completions. Select the one that BEST answers the question or completes the statement. *PRINT THE LETTER OF THE CORRECT ANSWER IN THE SPACE AT THE RIGHT.*

Questions 1-2.

DIRECTIONS: Questions 1 and 2 refer to the vertical curve shown below.

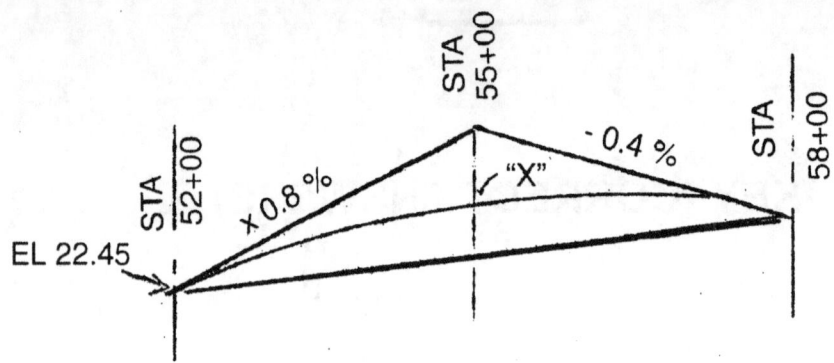

1. The algebraic difference in gradient between the two slopes is

   A. 0.6%   B. -0.8%   C. +1.0%   D. +1.2%

   1._____

2. The elevation of point X on the curve is

   A. 22.80'   B. 23.25'   C. 23.55'   D. 23.95'

   2._____

3. Plain concrete is USUALLY composed of

   A. cement, sand, and gravel
   B. cement and sand
   C. cement, crushed rock, and gravel
   D. gypsum and sand

   3._____

4. If a 100-feet-long steel tape expands 5/64" for a temperature rise of 10°F, then the expansion of a 91-feet-long steel tape with a temperature rise of 70°F is

   A. 3/8"   B. 1/2"   C. 3/4"   D. 7/8"

   4._____

5. Of the following, the one that is NOT used as a lightweight aggregate for concrete is

   A. cinders   B. traprock
   C. pumice   D. vermiculite

   5._____

6. In tunnel construction, the points that mark the center line of the tunnel are USUALLY set

   A. in the roof of the tunnel
   B. on the ground four feet off the center line of the tunnel
   C. on the ground at the center line of the tunnel
   D. on the side of the tunnel at center line elevation

   6._____

2 (#3)

7. The high rod reading shown at the right is
   A. 8.100
   B. 8.125
   C. 8.135
   D. 8.250

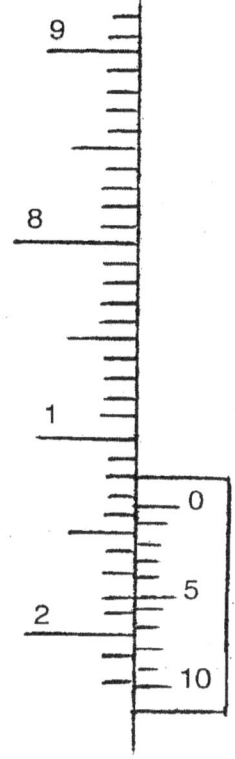

8. The value of 6!/72 is

   A. 10   B. 12   C. 14   D. 16

9. The fourth term of the binomial $(X+a)^5$ is

   A. $15a^4X^3$ B. $10a^3X^2$ C. a^5 D. $5aX^4$

10. If steel weighs 490 #/cu.ft., then the cross-sectional area, in square inches, of an 8[11.5 is MOST NEARLY

    A. 3.04   B. 3.22   C. 3.38   D. 3.45

11.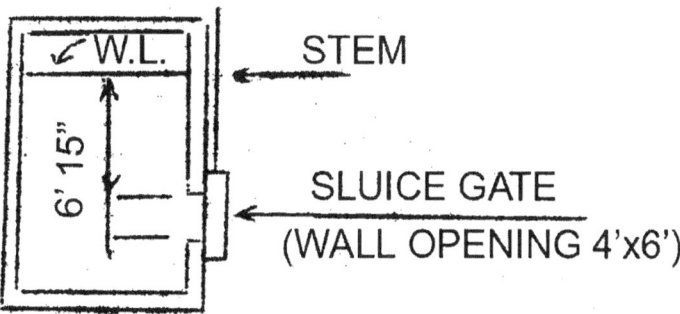

    The total horizontal water pressure, in pounds, acting on the above shown sluice gate is MOST NEARLY

    A. 23,000   B. 25,000   C. 27,000   D. 29,000

12. Terrazzo would MOST likely be found on

    A. ceilings   B. floors
    C. interior walls   D. exterior walls

13. In the laying out of a building foundation, batter boards are set   13.____

    A. outside the corners of the building
    B. inside the sides of the building
    C. inside diagonally opposite corners of the building only
    D. outside one side and inside one corner of the building only

14. The value of the determinant shown at the right is   14.____

    $\begin{vmatrix} 8 & 5 \\ 2 & 1 \end{vmatrix}$

    A. 37
    B. 16
    C. 10
    D. -2

15. If the product of the slopes of two lines is -1, then the lines are   15.____

    A. 30° to each other   B. perpendicular
    C. parallel   D. collinear

16. Blowoffs are provided on water mains to   16.____

    A. provide access to inspect the main
    B. remove sediment in the lines
    C. prevent the buildup of excessive pressure
    D. minimize the effect of water hammer

17. A 10-foot section of a 48" round sewer settles 6 inches.   17.____
    Of the following, the MOST probable consequence of this condition is the

    A. reduction in the carrying capacity of the pipe
    B. possibility of an air lock at this point
    C. stoppage of flow due to sediment
    D. possibility of cavitation in the pipe

18. The clearance of bridges over navigable waterways is the *official* concern of the   18.____

    A. Coast and Geodetic Survey
    B. Navy Department
    C. U.S. Army
    D. Department of the Interior

19. On a highway project, a test that is USUALLY performed to determine the compaction of   19.____
    the subbase is a _____ test.

    A. density   B. slump
    C. compression   D. grain size

20. Of the following, the statement that is CORRECT with respect to transverse joints in   20.____
    pavements is:
    A(n)

    A. expansion joint allows for both expansion and contraction
    B. contraction joint allows for both expansion and contraction
    C. warping joint allows for both expansion and contraction
    D. warping joint allows for both contraction and warping

21. The curve that facilitates the transition from the normal crowned straight section of a roadway to the banked curved section of roadway is known as a(n)

    A. spiral easement
    B. parabola
    C. simple circle
    D. hyperbola

    21.____

22. In trench excavation, a pair of vertical boards placed on opposite sides of a trench with two cross braces holding then is known as

    A. vertical sheeting
    B. poling boards
    C. box sheeting
    D. stay bracing

    22.____

23. The penetration test on asphalt cement is used to determine its

    A. density
    B. hardness
    C. elasticity
    D. time of set

    23.____

24. A concrete column with an effective cross-section 20 inches square has one percent vertical steel reinforcing with proper ties.
    Assuming fc = 500 pounds per square inch and n = 15, the capacity of the column for taking axial load, in pounds, is APPROXIMATELY (P = fc[1+(n-1)Po])

    A. 175,000 B. 200,000 C. 225,000 D. 250,000

    24.____

25. Turning of metals is USUALLY performed on a

    A. radial drill press
    B. lathe
    C. milling machine
    D. shaper

    25.____

KEY (CORRECT ANSWERS)

1. D
2. D
3. A
4. B
5. B
6. A
7. C
8. A
9. B
10. C

11. C
12. B
13. A
14. D
15. B
16. B
17. A
18. C
19. A
20. A

21. A
22. D
23. B
24. C
25. B

TEST 4

DIRECTIONS: Each question or incomplete statement is followed by several suggested answers or completions. Select the one that BEST answers the question or completes the statement. *PRINT THE LETTER OF THE CORRECT ANSWER IN THE SPACE AT THE RIGHT.*

1. An eighth of an inch is equal MOST NEARLY to _____ of a foot.

   A. 1/10   B. 1/100   C. 1/64   D. 1/84

2. In the sketch above, the type of internal stress acting on the member along line A-A due to the load P shown above is

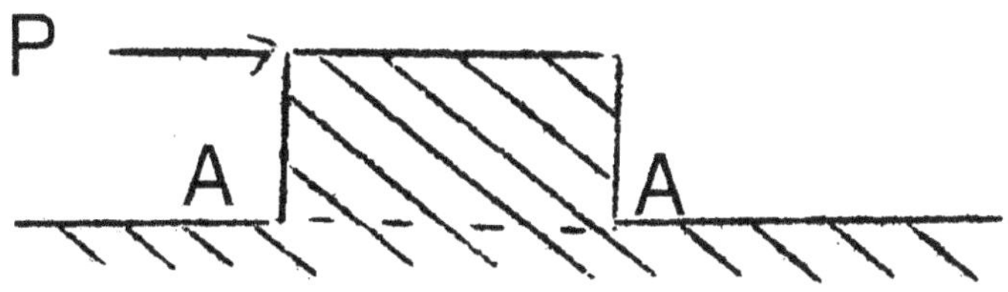

   A. tension and compression *only*
   B. tension and shear *only*
   C. tension, compression, and shear
   D. shear *only*

3. Lime used in mortar is USUALLY

   A. hydrated lime   B. quicklime
   C. unslaked lime   D. plaster of paris

4. An air entraining compound is PRIMARILY added to concrete to

   A. make it light
   B. make it set early
   C. eliminate the need for curing
   D. make it more durable

5. The arrangement of bricks shown at the right is _____ Bond.
   A. English
   B. Flemish
   C. Common
   D. Danish

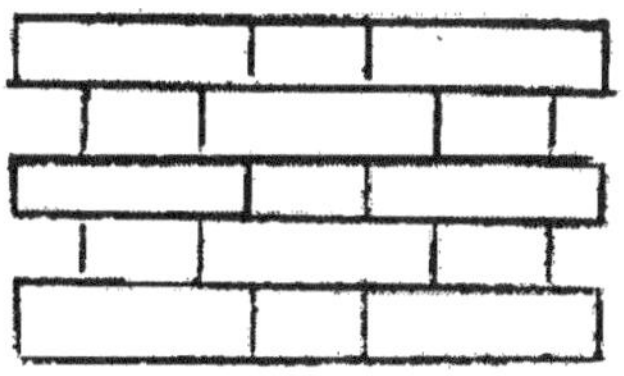

6. The coverage of a paint is 360 sq.ft./gallon.
   The number of gallons required to paint the walls of four rooris, 11'1" x 12'8" by 7'6" high, with one coat, is MOST NEARLY (do not count windows or doors)

   A. 2   B. 3   C. 4   D. 5

7. In the ELEVATION shown at the right, stone X is known as a
   A. reglet
   B. baffle
   C. perron
   D. coping

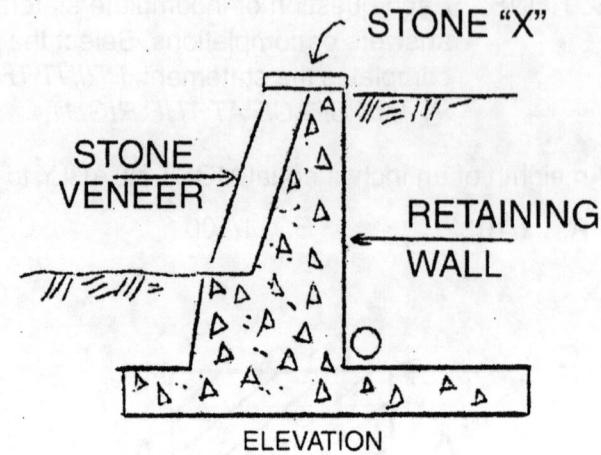

8. The material MOST commonly used as a conductor in ordinary electric wiring is
   A. brass   B. zinc   C. copper   D. aluminum

9. In trigonometry, the expression Cos X cos Y - Sin X sin Y
   A. Sin(X+Y)   B. Sin(X-Y)   C. Cos(X+Y)   D. Cos(X-Y)

10. In the window shown at the right, X is called a
    A. jamb
    B. muntin
    C. stool
    D. mullion

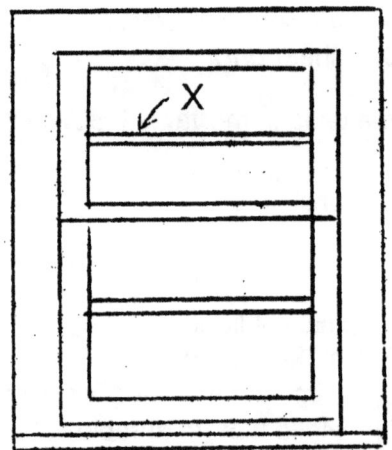

11. If the Sin X = .60, then the Cos X =
    A. .50   B. .60   C. .70   D. .80

12. The length of a meter is, in inches, MOST NEARLY
    A. 39.4   B. 38.6   C. 37.2   D. 36.9

13. To complete the square in the terms $X^2 + 10X$, we would have to add
    A. 20   B. 25   C. 30   D. 100

14. In the sketch shown at the right, the distance X - Y is MOST NEARLY
    A. 8'5"
    B. 8'8"
    C. 9'0"
    D. 9'3"

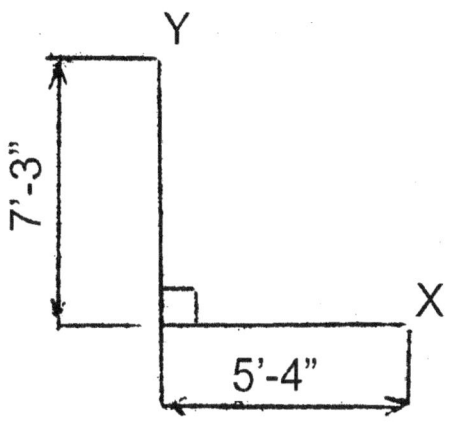

15. A rectangular footing is to have an area of 250 square feet. If the length is to be twice its width, then the width is MOST NEARLY

    A. 11.0'   B. 11.2'   C. 11.4'   D. 11.5'

16. In the term *4000 pound concrete*, the term *4000 pound*, as applied to ordinary concrete, represents the ultimate compressive strength of the concrete at the end of _____ days.

    A. 3   B. 7   C. 14   D. 28

17.

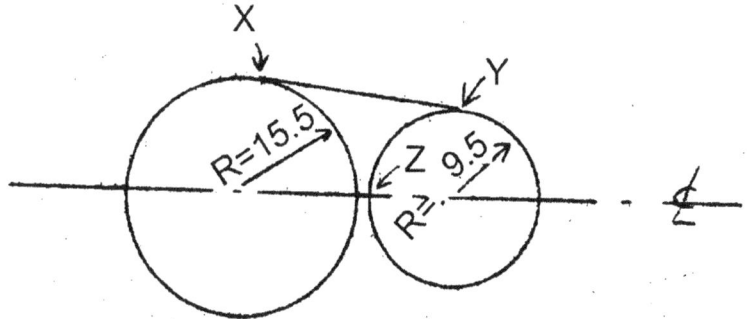

In the sketch shown above, the length of the common tangent XY to the two circles tangent at Z is

    A. 21.3   B. 22.3   C. 23.3   D. 24.3

18. $\sin(X+90)°$ is equal to

    A. Cos X   B. Sin X   C. - Cos X   D. - Sin X

19. In a contract that includes both unit-price and lump-sum items, the one that is LEAST likely to be bid on a unit-price basis is

    A. cleaning up
    B. seeding and mulching
    C. fencing
    D. waterstops

20. The PRIMARY reason for providing sewers with manholes is to

    A. ventilate the sewage
    B. clean and inspect the sewer
    C. connect future house connections
    D. allow sewer to surcharge

21. The number of radians in the arc of a circle having a central angle of 30° is   21._____

    A. π/6   B. π/5   C. π/4   D. π/3

22. The weight of a cubic foot of cement is, in pounds, MOST NEARLY   22._____

    A. 86   B. 90   C. 94   D. 98

23. The invert elevation at a manhole of a sewer is 65.40'. If the slope of the pipe is .0063 ft./   23._____
    ft., then the invert elevation at a manhole 275 ft. downstream is

    A. 63.25'   B. 63.67'   C. 63.85'   D. 63.98'

24. The cutting out of the top flange and web of a steel member so that the steel member will   24._____
    frame into another steel member is called

    A. coping   B. crimping   C. canting   D. corbelling

25. The architectural symbol [∧∧∧∧] is a section representing   25._____

    A. marble   B. glazed tile
    C. clay tile   D. insulation

KEY (CORRECT ANSWERS)

1. B		11. D	
2. C		12. A	
3. A		13. B	
4. D		14. C	
5. B		15. B	
6. C		16. D	
7. D		17. D	
8. C		18. A	
9. C		19. A	
10. B		20. B	

21. A
22. C
23. B
24. A
25. D

EXAMINATION SECTION
TEST 1

DIRECTIONS: Each question or incomplete statement is followed by several suggested answers or completions. Select the one that BEST answers the question or completes the statement. *PRINT THE LETTER OF THE CORRECT ANSWER IN THE SPACE AT THE RIGHT.*

1. $\sqrt{465}$ is MOST NEARLY

    A. 20.56　　B. 21.13　　C. 21.34　　D. 21.56

2. 90° is MOST NEARLY equal to _____ radians.

    A. 0.5　　B. 1.5　　C. 2.5　　D. 3.5

3. When .68 feet is converted to inches, the result is MOST NEARLY

    A. 7 7/8"　　B. 8"　　C. 8 1/8"　　D. 8 1/4"

4. A 100' guy wire, stretched tight from the top of a vertical pole, makes a 60° angle with the level ground.
   The height of this pole, in feet, is MOST NEARLY (sin 60° = .867, cos 60° = .500)

    A. 50　　B. 87　　C. 100　　D. 200

5. The area of a 120° sector of a circle whose radius is 3" is MOST NEARLY _____ square inches.

    A. 7.9　　B. 9.42　　C. 11.3　　D. 12.5

6. The product $\dfrac{6xy}{x^2-4} \cdot \dfrac{5x-10}{3xy}$ is equal to

    A. $\dfrac{2xy}{x^2-40}$　　B. $\dfrac{30x^2}{x^2 y}$　　C. $\dfrac{10}{x+2}$　　D. $\dfrac{18x^3 y}{x+10}$

7. The $\sin^2 x$ is equal to

    A. $1 - 2\cos^2 x$
    C. $1 + \cos^2 x$
    B. $1 + 2\cos^2 x$
    D. $1 - \cos^2 x$

8. The volume of a cylinder with a radius of r and height h is

    A. $\pi r^2 h$　　B. $2\pi rh$　　C. $2\pi r^2 h$　　D. $4\pi r^2 h$

9. The expression $\sqrt{28} - \sqrt{7}$ reduces to

    A. $\sqrt{7}$　　B. $3\sqrt{7}$　　C. $\sqrt{21}$　　D. $-\sqrt{35}$

10. If sin 2x = 1, then x is

    A. 30° B. 45° C. 60° D. 75°

11. The expression $\dfrac{x^{-2}y^2}{y} - \dfrac{x^2}{x^4} + y^0$ reduces to

    A. $\dfrac{xy}{x^4}$ B. $\dfrac{y^2}{y-x^4}$ C. $\dfrac{y-1}{x^2+1}$ D. $\dfrac{y-1}{x^2+y}$

12. If the coordinates of E and F in the X-Y plane are (1,-1) and (4,3), respectively, then the length of line E-F is

    A. 4 B. 5 C. 6 D. 7

13. The sum of the interior angles of a regular octagon is

    A. 360° B. 540° C. 1080° D. 1800°

14. The number of cubic yards of concrete required to fill eighteen 24" diameter steel pipe piles 150 feet long is MOST NEARLY

    A. 80 B. 155 C. 315 D. 630

15. A flow of 100 gallons per second for a day is, in millions of gallons per day, MOST NEARLY equal to

    A. 7.93 B. 8.05 C. 8.64 D. 9.20

16. It takes 4 hours for a certain pump to drain an excavation by itself. It takes a second pump 6 hours to drain that same excavation working by itself.
    If both pumps are used together, the length of time it will take to drain the excavation is MOST NEARLY _____ minutes.

    A. 120 B. 144 C. 300 D. 600

17. The area, in square yards, of a trapezoid which has an altitude of 81 feet perpendicular to two parallel sides which are 125 feet and 275 feet long, respectively, is MOST NEARLY

    A. 600 B. 1,800 C. 5,400 D. 10,400

18. The expression $\dfrac{7!}{180}$ reduces to

    A. 28 B. 56 C. 112 D. 224

19. If Log 2 = .3010 and Log 3 = .4771, then Log 324 is MOST NEARLY

    A. 1.9898 B. 2.2094 C. 2.5104 D. 2.6387

20. An isosceles right triangle has a(n) _____ angle.

    A. obtuse   B. 45°   C. 60°   D. 30°

21. The number of cubic yards of topsoil required to cover a rectangular tract of land 108 feet long by 96 feet wide to a depth of 6 inches is MOST NEARLY

    A. 192   B. 198   C. 215   D. 230

22. If the payment for steel is 25 cents per pound and a 1-inch-square bar 1 foot long weighs 3.4#, then the payment for a steel bar 2" x 4" in cross section 8' long is

    A. $8.10   B. $32.80   C. $16.40   D. $54.40

23. Expressed in degrees, 57° - 35' - 20" is MOST NEARLY

    A. 57.585   B. 57.587   C. 57.589   D. 57.591

24.

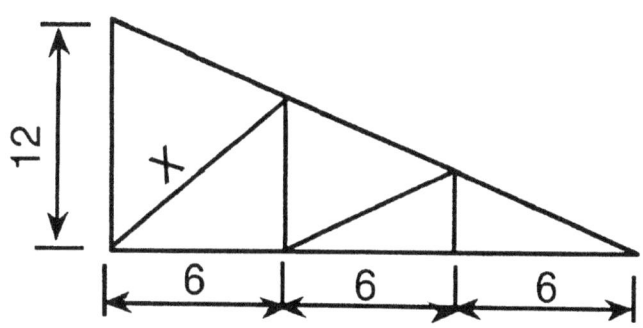

In the sketch shown above, the length of x is

    A. 8.0   B. 9.0   C. 9.5   D. 10.0

25. In Circle "O," inscribed angle ABC and central angle AOC have the same intercepted arc AC in common. Of the following relationships between angle AOC and angle ABC, the one which is TRUE is that

    A. angle ABC equals angle AOC
    B. angle AOC equals one-half angle ABC
    C. angle ABC equals one-half angle AOC
    D. nothing can be said about their relative sizes solely on the basis of the information given

KEY (CORRECT ANSWERS)

1.	D	11.	C
2.	B	12.	B
3.	C	13.	C
4.	B	14.	C
5.	B	15.	C
6.	C	16.	B
7.	D	17.	B
8.	A	18.	A
9.	A	19.	C
10.	B	20.	B

21. A
22. D
23. C
24. D
25. C

TEST 2

DIRECTIONS: Each question or incomplete statement is followed by several suggested answers or completions. Select the one that BEST answers the question or completes the statement. *PRINT THE LETTER OF THE CORRECT ANSWER IN THE SPACE AT THE RIGHT.*

1. In pounds per square inch above absolute 0, atmospheric pressure at sea level is MOST NEARLY

   A. 4.7 B. 14.7 C. 19.92 D. 29.92

   1.____

2. Of the following, the one that is a unit in which kinetic energy is expressed is

   A. feet
   B. foot pounds
   C. foot pounds/second
   D. foot pounds per second squared

   2.____

3. The formula for methane gas is

   A. CH_2 B. CH_4 C. C_2H_2 D. C_2H_4

   3.____

4. The substance represented by the formula PbS is known as

   A. galena   B. caustic soda
   C. zinc blende   D. litharge

   4.____

5. Of the following statements about water, the one which is TRUE is that

   A. it is practically incompressible
   B. it is most dense at 32° F
   C. a unit volume of water weighs less than the same volume of alcohol
   D. it has no surface tension

   5.____

6. A 50-ohm resistor and a 100-ohm resistor are connected in series to a 120-volt source. Heat will be developed

   A. in the 50-ohm resistor at a greater rate
   B. in the 100-ohm resistor at a greater rate
   C. in both resistors at the same rate
   D. at a greater rate in whichever resistor is connected to the positive side of the voltage source

   6.____

7. An object falling freely from rest for one-half second will drop a distance of MOST NEARLY _____ feet.

   A. 4 B. 8 C. 16 D. 32

   7.____

8. The horsepower required to lift a 2,200-pound weight a vertical distance of 3 feet in one-half second is MOST NEARLY (HP = $\frac{wh}{550}$)

   A. 3 B. 12 C. 24 D. 30

   8.____

93

9. When 2 amps flow through a 20-ohm resistor, the power dissipated by this resistor is MOST NEARLY _____ watts.

   A. 10 B. 20 C. 40 D. 80

10. When the velocity of an object following a circular path is doubled, the centripetal force necessary to keep it in its circular path is

    A. halved
    B. unchanged
    C. doubled
    D. quadrupled

11. The potential difference across a 3-ohm resistor is 12 volts. The current flowing through this resistor is MOST NEARLY _____ amps.

    A. 2 B. 4 C. 6 D. 27

12. The equivalent on the Fahrenheit scale of 100 degrees Centigrade is

    A. 100° B. 132° C. 180° D. 212°

13. Of the following, the chemical that is an organic compound is

    A. C_6H_6 B. HNO_3 C. H_2SO_3 D. SiO_2

14. A substance which changes the speed of a chemical reaction without itself being permanently changed is known as

    A. amorphous
    B. an amphoteric compound
    C. a catalyst
    D. a salt

15. A chemical reaction accompanied by the evolution of heat is known as

    A. an endothermic reaction
    B. an exothermic reaction
    C. neutralization
    D. nuclear fission

16. The mixing of gases, liquids, and solids by means of molecular motion is called

    A. diffusion
    B. effervescence
    C. decomposition
    D. filtration

17. The ideal mechanical advantage of the pulley system pictured at the right is MOST NEARLY

    A. 2
    B. 3
    C. 4
    D. 5

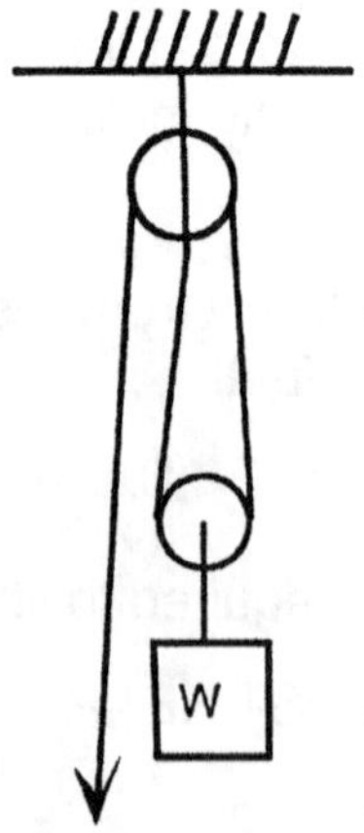

18. Of the following colors of light, the one with the LONGEST wavelength is

    A. red B. orange C. yellow D. blue

19.

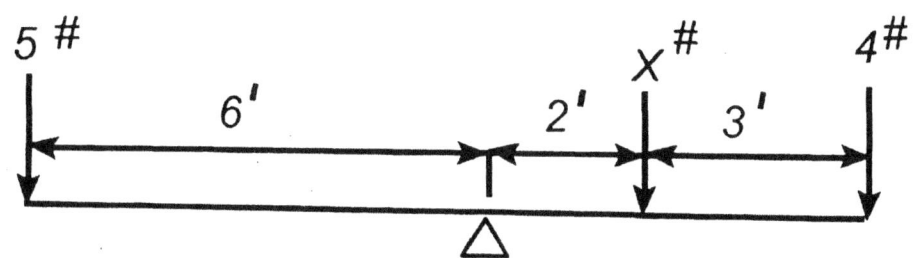

In the lever shown in the sketch above, the magnitude of force X needed to balance the lever is MOST NEARLY _____ lbs.

A. 3.0 B. 4.5 C. 5.0 D. 6.0

20. A 2-candlepower lamp is placed 2 ft. from a photometer screen. Another lamp placed 6 feet from the screen produces equal illumination on the screen.
The illumination of the second lamp is MOST NEARLY _____ cp.

A. 15 B. 18 C. 20 D. 25

21. If, in the diagram shown at the right, the bearing of line OY is S65° E, then the bearing of line OX is

A. S17° E
B. N17° E
C. N17° W
D. S17° W

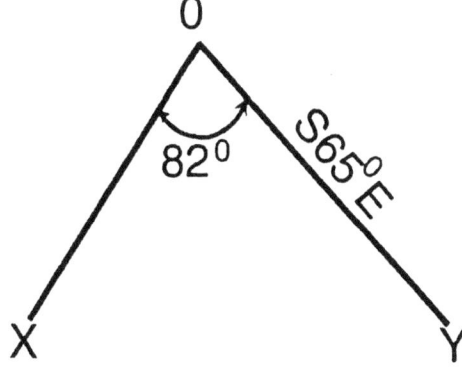

22. If a backsight on a benchmark whose elevation is 116.75' is 8.42' and the foresight on a turning point is 9.35', then the elevation of the turning point is

A. 119.71' B. 118.53' C. 117.68' D. 115.82'

23.

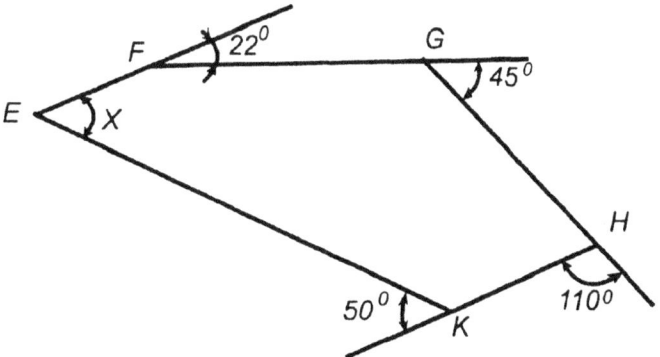

In the closed traverse shown above, the angle X is

A. 33° B. 40° C. 47° D. 55°

24. If a 100-foot-long steel tape contracts 0.00645' upon a temperature drop of 10° F, then the contraction of an 85-foot steel tape for a temperature drop of 65° F is MOST NEARLY

   A. 0.0223'   B. 0.0268'   C. 0.0301'   D. 0.0355'

25. A map made primarily to show relief in ground in such a manner that elevations may be obtained by inspection is known as a(n) _____ map.

   A. planimetric   B. isogonic
   C. railroad   D. topographic

KEY (CORRECT ANSWERS)

1. B
2. B
3. B
4. A
5. A
6. B
7. A
8. C
9. D
10. D
11. B
12. D
13. A
14. C
15. B
16. A
17. A
18. A
19. C
20. B
21. D
22. D
23. C
24. D
25. D

EXAMINATION SECTION
TEST 1

DIRECTIONS: Each question or incomplete statement is followed by several suggested answers or completions. Select the one that BEST answers the question or completes the statement. *PRINT THE LETTER OF THE CORRECT ANSWER IN THE SPACE AT THE RIGHT.*

1. If $x = 3$ and $3x^4 - x + 4x^0 - 3x^{-1} = y$, then y equals

    A. 81   B. 235   C. 240   D. 243

    1.____

2. If $\sqrt{x^2+9} - x = 1$, then x is

    A. 9   B. 5   C. 4   D. 2

    2.____

3. If $1/x = y + 1/2$, then x is equal to

    A. $\dfrac{z+1}{yz+1}$ B. $\dfrac{y^2}{z}$ C. y^2 D. $\dfrac{z}{yz+1}$

    3.____

4. The secant of $30°$ is

    A. $\dfrac{2}{\sqrt{3}}$ B. $\dfrac{\sqrt{3}}{2}$ C. $\dfrac{1}{\sqrt{2}}$ D. $\dfrac{-\sqrt{2}}{\sqrt{3}}$

    4.____

5. If $\sqrt{x} = \dfrac{y^2}{z}$, then y is equal to

    A. $x^2 y^2$ B. $xz^{\frac{3}{2}}$ C. $(x^2 z)^{\frac{1}{3}}$ D. $(xz^2)^{\frac{1}{4}}$

    5.____

6. The altitude of a triangle exceeds the base by 4 inches. If the area of the triangle is 30 square inches, the base and altitude of the triangle are _____ and _____ inches, respectively.

    A. 6; 10   B. 5; 12   C. 2; 6   D. 2; 30

    6.____

7. The value of $\dfrac{7!}{4!}$ is

    A. 30   B. 175   C. 210   D. 220

    7.____

8. If $2x = 3y$ and $4x - 5y = 2$, then x equals

    A. 6   B. 5   C. 4   D. 3

    8.____

9. Given the points A(-5,-1) and B(3,5), the length of line segment AB is

    A. 6 B. 10 C. 12 D. 25

10. The sum of the interior angles of a polygon with eight sides is

    A. 1260° B. 1080° C. 800° D. 720°

11. Assume that a stairway has 18 risers. Each riser is 7 1/2" high. If the floor elevation at the lower level is 102.00 feet, then the floor elevation at the upper level is MOST NEARLY _____ feet.

    A. 109.72 B. 112.10 C. 113.25 D. 114.05

12. The top course of a wall, designed to shed water and to give a finished appearance, is the

    A. jamb
    B. saddle
    C. water table
    D. coping

13. A map is drawn to a scale of 1" = 30'. The type of scale that would indicate distances on this map without further conversion is a(n)

    A. engineers scale
    B. architects scale
    C. surveyor's tape
    D. yard stick

14. If an isometric drawing has one axis vertical, then the other two axes make an angle with the horizontal equal to

    A. 30° B. 45° C. 60° D. 90°

15. The foundations of a building should be carried below the frost line to prevent

    A. pollution
    B. corrosion
    C. asphyxiation
    D. heaving

16. Creosote is COMMONLY used as a preservative for

    A. vitrified clay sewers
    B. brick walls
    C. PVC pipe
    D. timber piles

17. Gaseous chlorine is a greenish-yellow poisonous substance used in the disinfection of water. When used for disinfection, its PRIMARY purpose is to

    A. kill bacteria
    B. prevent corrosion
    C. filter the water
    D. color the water green

18. A bolt has a round head and a square nut. The portion of the shank immediately under the head is square and the remainder of the shank is round. This type of bolt is called a _____ bolt.

    A. carriage B. expansion C. lag D. toggle

19. The size of a nail is designated as 8d. This designation means

    A. 8 penny
    B. 8 times the diameter
    C. 8 inches
    D. 8 centimeters

20. Noxious gases and foul odors are prevented from passing from the sewer to the building drainage pipes by a

    A. cross connection
    B. goose neck
    C. wye fitting
    D. trap with a water seal

21. While trenches are being excavated, for sewer construction, the earth sides are frequently held in place by

    A. sheeting
    B. a cradle
    C. slope stakes
    D. batter boards

22. After concrete is poured, it is covered with plastic sheets or wet burlap in order to reduce

    A. evaporation
    B. vibration
    C. settlement
    D. honeycombing

23. A 1:2:4 concrete consists of 1 part cement to 2 parts fine aggregate and 4 parts

    A. gypsum
    B. lime
    C. water
    D. coarse aggregate

24. A sewer is laid on a slope of 0.25% between two manholes 180 feet apart. The difference in elevation between the upstream and downstream ends of the sewer is MOST NEARLY _____ feet.

    A. 0.45   B. 0.60   C. 0.90   D. 1.80

25. A map is drawn to a scale of 1" = 2000'.
    If 1 acre equals 43,560 square feet, then a 10 inch diameter circle on the map represents an area of MOST NEARLY _____ acres.

    A. 564   B. 3604   C. 4326   D. 7208

KEY (CORRECT ANSWERS)

1. D
2. C
3. D
4. A
5. D
6. A
7. C
8. D
9. B
10. B

11. C
12. D
13. A
14. A
15. D
16. D
17. A
18. A
19. A
20. D

21. A
22. A
23. D
24. A
25. D

TEST 2

DIRECTIONS: Each question or incomplete statement is followed by several suggested answers or completions. Select the one that BEST answers the question or completes the statement. *PRINT THE LETTER OF THE CORRECT ANSWER IN THE SPACE AT THE RIGHT.*

1. A plan is drawn to a scale of 3/8" = 1'0".
   A line 2 1/2" long on the plan represents a distance of MOST NEARLY _____ feet.

   A. 9.21   B. 8.00   C. 7.33   D. 6.67

2. Two gears of different diameters are meshed together. If the larger gear rotates at 100 rpm, the SMALLER gear will rotate

   A. faster
   B. slower
   C. at the same speed
   D. first in one direction, then in the other

3. A fence is to be constructed along the property lines of a rectangular tract 60' x 100'. One fence post is to be placed at each corner, and the rest of the posts are to be placed around the periphery, at 10' on centers. Neglecting gates, the number of fence posts required is

   A. 38   B. 36   C. 34   D. 32

4. A piece of wood 2 feet thick, 1 foot wide, and 10 feet long weighs 800 pounds. The wood is placed in water weighing 62.4 pounds per cubic foot.
   If the 2-foot-by-10-foot side is parallel to the surface of the water, the 1-foot side will be submerged to a depth of MOST NEARLY _____ inches.

   A. 6.24   B. 7.10   C. 7.39   D. 7.69

5. Drawings for a building are made on sheets 36" x 48". There are 120 drawings in a set. If prints cost 6 cents per square foot, the cost for three prints of each of the 120 drawings is MOST NEARLY

   A. $259   B. $230   C. $99   D. $52

6. Of the following, the one which would NOT be used for sub-surface examination is

   A. auger borings   B. test pits
   C. core borings   D. stadia measurements

7. The diary of a construction project is MOST commonly known as a

   A. log   B. organization chart
   C. bar diagram   D. audit

8. On a topographic map, a contour line is a line joining points of EQUAL

   A. temperature   B. distance   C. pressure   D. elevation

9. If there are 43,560 square feet in an acre and 640 acres in a square mile, then the number of acres in a tract of land 2640 feet by 7920 feet is MOST NEARLY

   A. 640   B. 480   C. 360   D. 10

101

10. Point B is 3 miles north and 4 miles east of Point A. A person traveling in a straight line from A to B and back again to A would travel a distance EQUAL to ___ miles.

    A. 14   B. 12   C. 10   D. 5

11. The flow from a wide open fire hydrant is 300 gallons per minute. When the hydrant is equipped with a spray nozzle, the flow is reduced to 20 gallons per minute.
    Over a period of 8 hours, the quantity of water saved by installing a spray nozzle is MOST NEARLY _____ gallons.

    A. 146,200   B. 134,400   C. 56,500   D. 2,400

12. A rectangular building is 100 feet long and 40 feet wide. Waterproofing is to be applied to the exterior of the 10-foot high basement walls at the rate of 2.5 gallons per 100 square feet of wall.
    The number of gallons of waterproofing required is MOST NEARLY

    A. 70   B. 60   C. 28   D. 10

13. An angle is measured 4 times, and the total of the four readings is 186 41' 22".
    The angle is MOST NEARLY

    A. 47 10' 12.0"   B. 46 40' 20.5"
    C. 46 32' 17.6"   D. 45 30' 15.4"

14. A wood beam spans 20 feet. A man weighing 150 pounds stands 4 feet from the left support, and a man weighing 200 pounds stands 10 feet from the left support. Neglecting the weight of the beam, the reaction at the left support is MOST NEARLY _____ pounds.

    A. 350   B. 250   C. 220   D. 200

15. A car starting from rest accelerates at the rate of 10 ft/sec^2.
    At the end _____ of 6 seconds, the distance the car will have traveled is MOST NEARLY _____ feet.

    A. 322   B. 180   C. 155   D. 60

16. The bearing of line EF is S30°W, and the bearing of line EG is N80°W.
    The angle CEF is MOST NEARLY

    A. 120°   B. 80°   C. 70°   D. 60°

17. A machine lifts a steel beam weighing 5000 pounds to the top of a building 44 feet high in 40 seconds.
    If 55 ft. lbs/sec is equal to one horsepower, the horsepower developed in lifting the beam is MOST NEARLY

    A. 35   B. 24   C. 18   D. 10

18. The distance on a survey line between station 107 + 21.2 and 3 + 72.8 is MOST NEARLY _____ feet.

    A. 7093.4   B. 10347.4   C. 10348.4   D. 10783.9

19. A stone weighs 160 pounds in air and 100 pounds when submerged in water which weighs 62.4 pounds per cubic foot.
    The volume of the stone is MOST NEARLY _____ cubic feet.

    A. 0.44   B. 0.82   C. 0.86   D. 0.96

20. A square tract of land contains 57,600 square feet. The length of a fence needed to enclose the entire property is MOST NEARLY _____ feet.

    A. 960   B. 752   C. 480   D. 300

21. The number of board feet in a piece of wood 1" x 12" x 10' is MOST NEARLY

    A. 0.83   B. 10   C. 12   D. 120

22.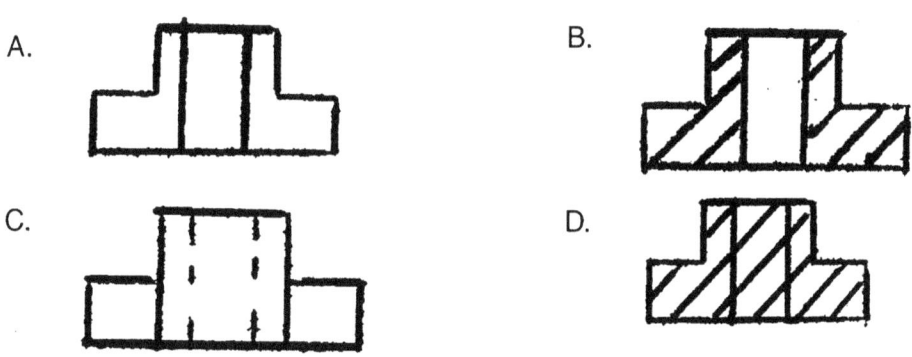

PLAN

The plan of an object is shown above. Section X - X should be shown as

A. B. C. D.

Questions 23-25.

DIRECTIONS: Questions 23 through 25 are to be answered on the basis of the top view and front elevation of an object as shown at the left. At the right are four drawings, one of which represents the end elevation of the object as seen from the right. Select the drawing which represents the correct end elevation and put the correct letter in the space at the right.

The first group is shown as an example only. The correct answer is B.

4 (#2)

SAMPLE END ELEVATION

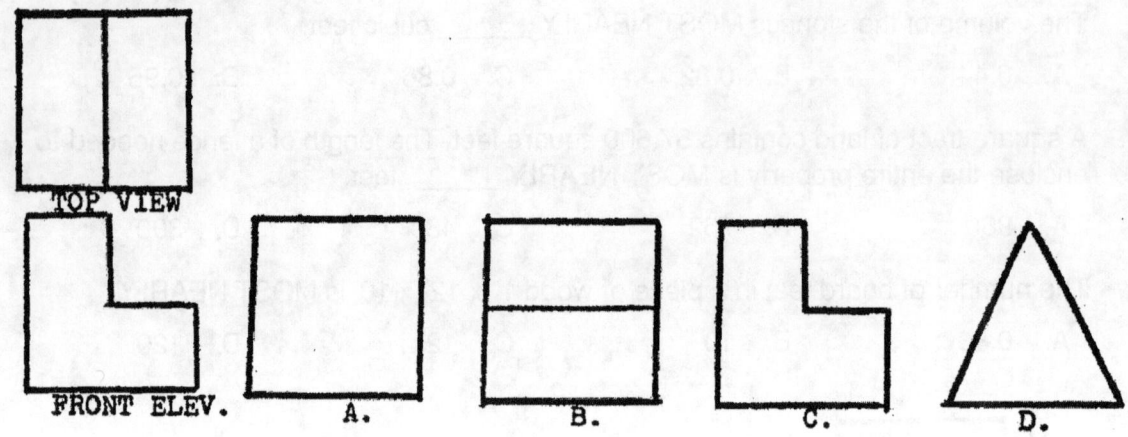

23.

24.

25.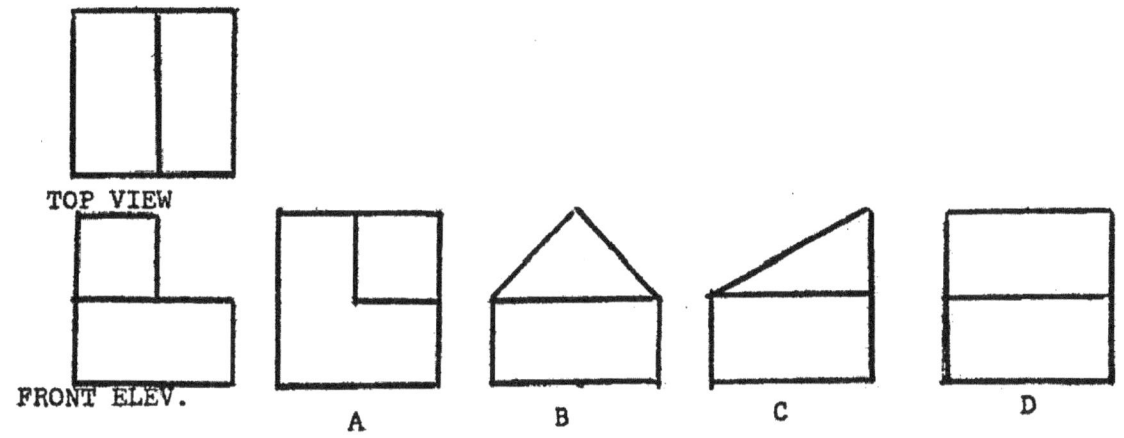

KEY (CORRECT ANSWERS)

1.	D	11.	B
2.	A	12.	A
3.	D	13.	B
4.	D	14.	C
5.	A	15.	B
6.	D	16.	C
7.	A	17.	D
8.	D	18.	C
9.	B	19.	D
10.	C	20.	A

21. B
22. B
23. A
24. B
25. C

EXAMINATION SECTION
TEST 1

DIRECTIONS: Each question or incomplete statement is followed by several suggested answers or completions. Select the one that BEST answers the question or completes the statement. *PRINT THE LETTER OF THE CORRECT ANSWER IN THE SPACE AT THE RIGHT.*

1. A planimeter is an instrument used to measure

    A. areas   B. angles   C. distances   D. elevations

2. In structural steel details, a line passing through the center of a row of rivets is called a(n) _____ line.

    A. section   B. extension   C. gage   D. cut

3. In topographic maps, the lines drawn to show relief by means of hill shading are called

    A. hachures   B. soundings   C. grid lines   D. flats

4. The projection of a circular cross-section, such as on a casting or forging, is called a

    A. bore   B. chamfer   C. core   D. boss

5. On a diagrammatic piping drawing, the symbol USUALLY indicates a

    A. check valve   B. union
    C. cross   D. 90 elbow

6. The welding symbol USUALLY indicates a _____ weld.

    A. bead   B. plug   C. fillet   D. groove

7. On an electrical wiring diagram, the symbol USUALLY indicates a

    A. junction box   B. ceiling outlet
    C. power panel   D. convenience outlet

8. A map is drawn to a scale of 1" = two miles. The distance between two points on the map is 2 1/2".
   The ACTUAL distance between the same two points on the ground is MOST NEARLY _____ feet.

    A. 25,200   B. 25,800   C. 26,400   D. 30,000

9. A topographic map is drawn to a scale of 1" = 200', with a contour interval of 2 feet. On a slope of 10%, the distance on the map between contours is MOST NEARLY _____ inches.

    A. 0.20   B. 0.15   C. 0.10   D. 0.05

10. The profile of a sewer is drawn to a scale of 1" = 50' Horizontal and 1" = 10' Vertical. The invert of the sewer drops 1.200 feet in a horizontal distance of 250 feet.
The actual slope of the sewer is MOST NEARLY

    A. 0.40%   B. 0.48%   C. 0.54%   D. 0.60%

11. When graph paper with logarithmically spaced rulings in both directions is used, an equation in which K and N are constants will plot as a straight line if it is of the form

    A. $y = \dfrac{K}{\log X} + \log N$ B. $y = KX^N$
    C. $y = K(\log X) + N$ D. $y = N(\log X) + K$

12. The distance between two trusses or transverse bents in a building is USUALLY called a

    A. set back   B. story   C. bay   D. chase

13. The CORRECT right side view of the object whose top and front views are as shown on the right is

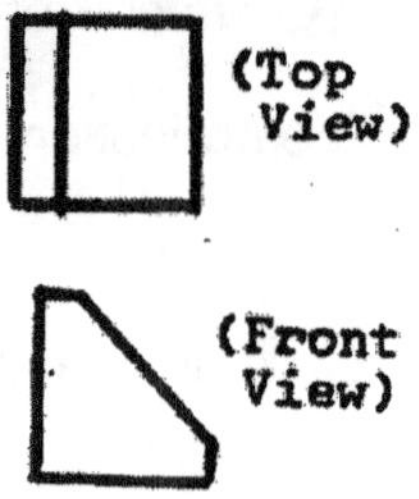

14. The CORRECT right side view of the object whose top and front views are as shown on the right is

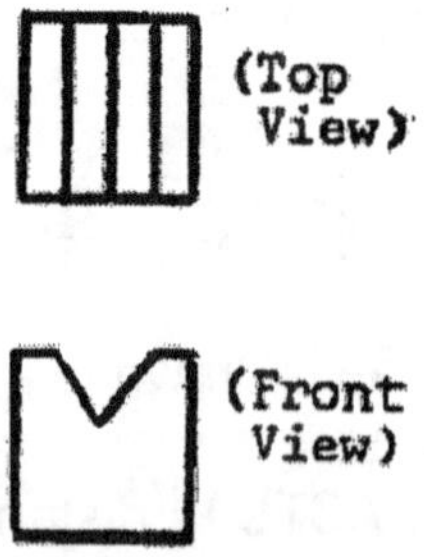

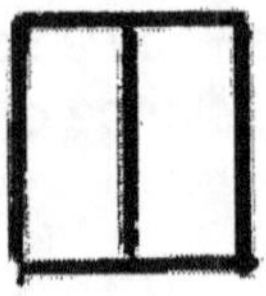

15. The CORRECT right side view of the object whose top and front views are as shown on the right is

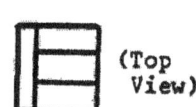 (Top View)

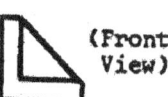 (Front View)

A.  B.  C.  D.

16. The CORRECT right side view of the object whose top and front views are as shown on the right is

 (Top View)

 (Front View)

A.  B.  C.  D.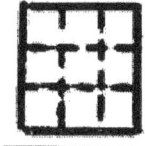

17. The expression $\left(\dfrac{T^6}{27}\right)^{1/3}$ is equivalent to

A. $\dfrac{T^2}{3}$ B. $\dfrac{T^{2/3}}{9}$ C. $\dfrac{T^{18}}{3}$ D. $\dfrac{T^{1/2}}{9}$

18. The fraction $\dfrac{(R-\frac{R}{t})}{(\frac{1}{t})-1}$ is equal to

A. R   B. 1/R   C. -R   D. -Rt

19. In triangle ABC, β =8, a = 9, and C = 135. The area of triangle ABC is   19.____

    A. 36   B. 30   C. $36\sqrt{2}$ D. $18\sqrt{2}$

20. Function y varies inversely as x. If y = 1 when x = 9, then when x = 3, y is equal to   20.____

    A. 2   B. 3   C. 12   D. 18

KEY (CORRECT ANSWERS)

1.	A	11.	B
2.	C	12.	C
3.	A	13.	B
4.	D	14.	D
5.	A	15.	A
6.	C	16.	C
7.	D	17.	A
8.	C	18.	C
9.	C	19.	D
10.	B	20.	B

TEST 2

DIRECTIONS: Each question or incomplete statement is followed by several suggested answers or completions. Select the one that BEST answers the question or completes the statement. *PRINT THE LETTER OF THE CORRECT ANSWER IN THE SPACE AT THE RIGHT.*

1. If the product of 0.02 and 0.0003 is written in the form 6×10^n, the value of n is   1.____
    A. -3   B. -4   C. -5   D. -6

2. The value of $\sqrt{275.56}$ is   2.____
    A. 15.8   B. 16.2   C. 16.6   D. 16.9

3. The sum of the interior angles of a polygon is 1620. The number of sides of the polygon is   3.____
    A. 9   B. 10   C. 11   D. 12

4. The angles of a triangle are in the ratio of 3:5:7. The number of degrees in the SMALLEST angle of the triangle is   4.____
    A. 24   B. 30   C. 36   D. 45

5. The line $2y = 6x + 4$ intersects the x axis at   5.____
    A. 2   B. 3/2   C. -1/2   D. -2/3

6. The cosine of 210° is   6.____
    A. $\frac{1}{2}$ B. $\frac{\sqrt{3}}{2}$ C. $\frac{-\sqrt{3}}{2}$ D. $\frac{-\sqrt{1}}{2}$

7. The coordinates of point A are (-3,-2) and the coordinates of point B are (2,10). The length of line AB is   7.____
    A. 18   B. 13   C. 10   D. 6

8. In the function $y = 4x^3 - 2x^2 + x^{-1}$, when $x = -2$, the value of y is   8.____
    A. 40 1/2   B. 24 1/2   C. -6 1/2   D. -40 1/2

9. The number of degrees in 1.5π radians is   9.____
    A. A.300   B. B.270   C. C.240   D. D.180

10. f $\log_{10} y = 3$, y equals   10.____
    A. 2.718   B. 100   C. 1000   D. 1122

11. One angle of a right angle triangle is 45°. If the perimeter is 16, the length of the hypotenuse is MOST NEARLY   11.____
    A. 5.42   B. 6.63   C. 7.89   D. 12.50

12. The expression (10a² - 3a - 18) divided by (5a+6) is equal to

    A. (2a+3)   B. (3a-2)   C. (3a+2)   D. (2a-3)

13. A 2" x 10" wood joist is horizontal and spans 12 feet. If the 10" side is vertical, the moment of inertia of the joist about a horizontal axis through the center of gravity is MOST NEARLY

    A. 137"⁴   B. 167"⁴   C. 197"⁴   D. 227"⁴

14. he rate o| flow over a weir is given by the formula $Q = 3.33bh^{3/2}$. When b = 10 and h = 4, the rate of flow, Q, is MOST NEARLY

    A. 234   B. 240   C. 252   D. 266

15. A concrete sidewalk 6 feet wide is to be constructed around a circular swimming pool. If the inside diameter of the sidewalk is 50 feet, the surface area of the sidewalk is MOST NEARLY

    A. 955 ft.²   B. 1055 ft.²   C. 1155 ft²   D. 1255 ft.²

16. A horizontal board 10 feet long is supported at each end. When a man stands on the board 3 feet from the right support, the right reaction, neglecting the weight of the board, is 140 pounds.
    If this man stood at the center of the board, the right reaction, neglecting the weight of the board, would be pounds.

    A. 120   B. 110   C. 100   D. 90

17. Water flows through an 8 inch diameter pipe at the rate of 1000 gpm. If 7.48 gals = 1 cu.ft., the average velocity in the pipe is _____ ft./sec.

    A. 9.11   B. 8.02   C. 7.41   D. 6.39

18. A concrete retaining wall is 150 feet long and 12 feet high. The cross-section is trapezoidal with a base of 24 inches and a top width of 12 inches.
    The volume of the wall is MOST NEARLY _____ cubic yards.

    A. 90   B. 100   C. 110   D. 120

19. A cantilever beam 12 feet long carries a uniformly distributed load of 300 pounds per foot including the weight of the beam.
    The bending moment at the support is _____ foot/pounds.

    A. 18400   B. 20400   C. 21600   D. 22600

20. A shaft rotates at 120 rpm and delivers 20 horsepower.
    If 550 ft. lbs. per second equals one horsepower, the torque in the shaft is MOST NEARLY _____ foot/pounds.

    A. 76   B. 80   C. 88   D. 94

KEY (CORRECT ANSWERS)

1. D
2. C
3. C
4. C
5. D

6. C
7. B
8. D
9. B
10. C

11. B
12. D
13. B
14. D
15. B

16. C
17. D
18. B
19. C
20. C

GLOSSARY OF CAD/DRAFTING TERMS

2D plane: A flat, infinite 2D surface.

A

active standard: The standard that is currently in use in a model or drawing file.

aligned dimension: A dimension used to define an object or feature that is not vertical or horizontal.

alt-drag: Establishing assembly constraints, including mate, flush, tangent, and insert constraints, by dragging one component to another component; also called *drag-mate*.

angular dimension: A dimension used to define the angle between two lines.

arc: A circular curve in which all of the points are an equal distance from the center point.

arrowless dimensioning: A dimensioning method that provides coordinates from established datum's those are usually located at the corner of the part or the axis of a feature. Also called *rectangular coordinate dimensioning without dimension lines* or ordinate dimensioning.

assembly: A grouping of one or more design components.

assembly drawing: A 2D representation of an assembly.

assembly constraints: Constraints that establish geometric relationships and positions between one component face, edge, or axis and another component face, edge, or axis.

auxiliary view: A view used to show the true size and shape of an inclined surface that is not parallel to any of the projected views, including the front, top, bottom, left-side, right-side, and back views.

axis of rotation: The pivot point around which the selected geometry is copied.

B

balloon: A shape, usually circular, that is connected to an assembly component by a leader. It contains an identification number or letter that refers to an item in the parts list.

base environment: The overall working environment, within which secondary environments exist.

base feature: The initial model feature, on which all others are based.

baseline dimensioning: A dimensioning method in which the size and location of features are given in reference to a datum. Also referred to as *datum dimensioning*.

base view: The first view placed in a drawing, to which all other views are added.

bend radius: The inside radius of a formed feature.

bend relief: Relief typically added to a sheet metal part to relieve stress, or the tear, that occurs when a portion of a piece of material is bent.

bent: Formed using a brake, die, mandrel, roller, or similar tools.

border: A rectangle or polygon near the edge of the drawing sheet that defines the usable drawing area of the drawing sheet. Borders may also include zone numbers and center marks.

boundary patch: A surface formed by patching the space within a selected closed region.

bowtie grips: Handlebar endpoints used to adjust the shape of a spline.

browser bar (browser): A panel that displays all the items in the current model or drawing.

C

cascading menu: A secondary menu that contains options related to the chosen menu item.

catalog feature: A feature, part, or assembly stored in a catalog that can be inserted into a part model as a feature.

centerline: A line that defines an axis of symmetry or the center of a circular feature.

center of gravity: The center of model mass, where balance occurs.

center point: The intersection point of the X, Y, and Z axes in 3D space, or 0,0,0.

chamfers: Angled planar faces added to lines or curves. Angled planar faces placed on a feature edge.

child node: Subordinate nodes that create, are associated with, or are consumed by the parent node item.

circular feature pattern: Occurrences of features copied and positioned a specified distance apart around an axis.

circular pattern: An arrangement of copies of a feature around an imaginary circle, a designated number of times, and at a specified distance apart.

circumscribed: Describes a polygon in which the flats are tangent to an imaginary circle; circumscribed polygons are measured across the polygon flats.

closed loop: A sketch that is fully closed and does not contain any gaps or openings.

coil: A spiral, or helix, feature used primarily to create springs, detailed threads, and similar items.

coincident constraint: A constraint that forces two points to share the same location.

combs: Lines added to the spline to help illustrate and analyze the spline curvature.

components: The individual parts and subassemblies used to create an assembly.

composite iMates: Two or more iMates linked together and added to a single component; used for the same assembly operation.

constant fillets and rounds: Fillets and rounds that have a curve radius that does not change.

constraints: Parameters that control the size, location, and position of model elements, including sketches and features. Restrictions applied to sketches to define sketch geometry in reference to other sketch geometry. Also called *geometric constraints*.

construction geometry: Geometry used for construction purposes only. Inventor cannot use construction geometry to build sketched features.

consumed: Used up in the creation of a model or feature.

context-sensitive shortcut menu: Menu in which only items associated with the current work environment and application are available.

control keys: Shortcut key combinations that include the [Ctrl] key and a character key.

coordinate system: The system of XYZ coordinate values that defines the location of points in 3D space.

corner chamfers: Angled faces that replace square corners on sheet metal features.

corner relief: Relief typically added to a sheet metal part to relieve stress at a bend corner at the intersection of two or three faces.

corner rip: A feature that opens closed, usually square, corners.

corner round: A curve placed at an inside or outside sheet metal corner.

corner seams: Features that add or remove material to form a gap at sheet metal part corners. Corner seams create an appropriate corner transition for folding and to allow for unfolding.

counter bored hole: A drilled hole that has a larger-diameter cylindrical opening at the top; typically used when a flush surface is necessary, such as to hide a binding screw head.

countersunk hole: Similar to a counter bored hole, but the recess is tapered, resulting in a conical shape that is often used to hide a screw head.

curve: A straight or bent continuous object, such as a line, arc, spline, or circle.

cut: Remove volume from an existing extrusion by subtracting a new extrusion from it. Any process, such as shearing, punching, or laser, water jet, or similar process, used to remove material.

cutting-plane line: A line that represents the cutting plane of the section, which is the location where the view is sliced to show interior features.

cutting tool: A surface, quilt, 2D sketch curve, work plane or existing feature face intersecting the surface to trim that provides an edge to which the item is trimmed.

D

dangling geometry: A condition that results when additional positioning information is required in order for iFeature insertion to occur; primarily due to issues with the initial iFeature sketch and existing feature geometry.

database: A system that stores every model characteristic, including calculations, sketches, features, dimensions, geometric constraints, when each piece of the model was created, and all other model parameters and properties.

datum: A theoretically exact point, axis, or plane from which the location or geometric characteristics of features originate.

datum dimensioning: A dimensioning method in which the size and location of features are given in reference to a datum. Also referred to as *baseline dimensioning*.

decals: Images applied to a part or assembly to display information or decoratea product.

demote: Group more than one part in an assembly to create a subassembly.

dependents: Assembly component files referenced by the assembly.

dependent views: Views projected from and linked to another view, such as a base view.

derived components: Features that can contain a complete model consisting of several features, or even multiple parts; often used as a base feature. A saved part or assembly that can be inserted in a part as a feature.

design session: Time spent working on a project, including analyzing design parameters and using Inventor.

detail view: A view that shows a small, complex part feature at a larger scale.

dialog box: A window-like part of the user interface that contains various kinds of information and settings.

diameter: The distance across a circle from one side to the other through the center.

diameter dimension: A dimension used to define the diameter of a circle or circular object.

dimension: A measurement that numerically defines the size and location of sketch geometry, such as the length of a line, diameter of a circle, or radius of an arc. Specifications of the size and shape of object features so that parts can be manufactured; along with notes and other text, also specify the location and characteristics of geometry and surface texture.

docked: Describes interface items that are locked into position on an edge of the Inventor window (top, bottom, left, or right).

document units: The units used to define the linear, angular, time, and mass measurements and precision in models and drawings.

double bend: A bend between two parallel faces that are not coplanar.

drag-mate: Establishing assembly constraints, including mate, flush, tangent, and insert constraints, by dragging one component to another component; also called *alt-drag*.

drawing annotation tools: Tools that allow you to create annotations such as dimensions, notes, and other text on drawings.

drawing dimensions: Dimensions added to the drawing using Inventor's drawing annotation tools.

drawing sheet: A representation of the physical limits of the paper size on which the drawing will be printed.

drawings: 2D representations of models containing views, dimensions, and annotations.

drilled hole: The most basic hole type, with no counterbore, spotface, or countersink where the hole begins.

driven: Manipulated to see the amount of movement between components, pause movement, see adaptivity, and detect collisions between components.

driven dimension: A dimension used for reference purposes only. Reference dimensions are enclosed in parentheses to show that they are driven.

E

ellipse: An oval-like shape that contains both a major axis and a minor axis.

embossing: The process of raising shapes or text off the surface of an object that has volume, such as a block; the opposite of engraving.

engraving: The process of cutting into, or impressing, shapes or text into the surface of an object that has volume; the opposite of embossing.

external threads: Thread forms on an external feature such as a pin, shaft, bolt, or screw.

extrusion: A surface or solid that has a fixed cross-sectional profile determined by a sketch profile. The sketch profile is extended (extruded) along a linear path to create the 3D feature or part.

F

face draft: A taper placed on a part surface.

feature pattern: An arrangement of copied existing features, generating occurrences of the features. An arrangement of features in a specific pattern, or configuration; created using feature pattern tools.

fillets: Rounded interior corners; fillets add material to corners. A curve placed at the inside intersection of two or more faces, adding material to a feature.

flat angle: The number of degrees a coil end travels without pitch.

flat end: A type of coil end in which the first or last coil is adjusted to create a flat start or finish for the spring.)

flat pattern: A 2D drawing representing the final, unfolded part.

floating: Describes interface items, displayed within a border, that can be freely resized or moved.

flush solution: A constraint that positions two faces along the same plane, facing the same direction.

flyout: A button that presents additional, related tool buttons, much like a cascading menu.

fly-through: A viewing process that shows how it would look if you could fly in and around the actual product you are modeling.

frequently used subfolder: A virtual folder within a project that stores the paths to folders and files you use frequently.

fully constrained model: A model that has no freedom of movement.

full radius fillets and rounds: Fillets and rounds controlled by the linear dimension of a feature, such as the thickness of a part or width of a slot, producing half of a circle or cylinder; most often associated with a round.

G

general notes: Notes that apply to the entire drawing. General notes are usually placed together in the lower-left or upper-right corner of the drawing or in the title block.

geometric constraints: Restrictions applied to sketches to define sketch geometry in reference to other sketch geometry. Also called *constraints*.

geometric dimensioning and tolerancing (GD&T): The dimensioning and tolerancing of individual features of a part where the permissible variations relate to characteristics of form, profile, orientation, runout, or the location of features.

grab bars: Two thin bars at the top or left edge of a docked or floating item; used to move the item.

graphical user interface (GUI): On-screen interface items.

grounded component: An assembly component that is fixed in position, has no freedom of movement, and cannot be driven.

grounded work point: A work point completely fixed to an X, Y, Z coordinate at which it is placed.

guide rail: A 2D or 3D sketched curve that is used with the sweep path to manipulate and further control the shape of a sweep.

guide surface: A surface that helps control

the shape of a sweep along a complex path.

H

height: In a coil, the total depth of the coil from the center of the starting profile to the center of the ending profile.

help string: A short description of what happens if you select a tool or option over which the cursor is hovering, or if a tool is selected, a prompt indicating the appropriate action is shown.

hem: Flanges used to add strength to or relieve the sharpness of exposed edges, or to connect separate edges or parts together.

hot keys: Single character keys on the keyboard that allow you to access certain predefined tools.

I

icon: A small graphic representing an application, file, or tool.

i-drop: The process of dragging and dropping shared content into component files, or the tool used for this process.

iFeature: An existing feature or set of features you create and then save and store in a catalog to be used in other models. A stored feature that can be inserted in a part as a feature.

iMates: Constraints placed on an individual component that are later used for assembly.

included angle: The angle between two selected edges, curves, axes, faces, planes, or a combination of objects, such as an edge and a face.

included file: A separate project file linked to the current project.

increment: A set amount by which values increase in equal steps. For example, with an increment of 2, a size would increase to 4, 6, 8, 10, and so on.

inferred: Automatically detected using logic.

inscribed: Describes a polygon in which the corners touch an imaginary circle; inscribed polygons are measured from the corners.

interface: The tools and techniques used to provide information to and receive information from a computer application. Also called a *user interface*.

internal threads: Thread forms on an internal hole feature.

iProperties: Inventor file properties used to define a variety of file and design characteristics.

isometric view: A 3D view in which all three axes are shown at equal angles (120°) with the plane of projection.

J

join: Combine two or more existing features to create a single feature.

K

k-factor: A multiple, typically between .25 and .5, that locates the neutral axis.

L

leader: A line that connects the beginning or end of a note to the feature it describes. Leaders usually have a horizontal shoulder on the end nearest the text. The other end has an arrow pointing to the feature.

left-hand threads: Threads that move a left-hand threaded bolt forward in a counterclockwise direction.

library: A folder that contains files used in a project or several different projects.

library search paths: The locations in which Inventor looks for library files on the computer's hard drive or on the network.

linear dimension: A type of dimension used to define the vertical and horizontal size and location of object features.

local notes: Notes that apply to a specific feature or features on the drawing. Also called *specific notes*.

loft: A feature that references and blends two or more sections located on different planes.

loft centerline: A rail that acts as a path for blending sections along and symmetrically around the centerline sketch.

lump: Any set of external feature or surface faces created when you develop a solid model.

M

mate solution: A constraint that places two faces along the same plane facing in opposite directions, two axes collinear to each other, two edges collinear to each other, or two points matched together.

mirrored feature: mirrored features: A mirror image of an existing feature created symmetrically over a specified plane.

mirror plane: A plane of symmetry about which features are mirrored.

miter gap: Space between faces created during a corner seam or miter operation.

model dimensions: Dimensions that were used to create and constrain the model from which drawing content has been extracted.

modeling failure: The result of conflicting constraints that are impossible to apply to the model.

model parameters: Parameters that relate to the model. Model parameters are added when you insert a model view or add model information, such as dimensions.

model space: A space, or environment, in which the model defines the display orientation, regardless of the position of the model in the graphics window; the center is associated with the model pivot point.

monodetail drawing: A drawing of a single part on one sheet.

motion constraints: Assembly constraints that identify how movable components should move in reference to other movable components, using a specified ratio and direction.

multidetail drawing: A drawing of several parts on one sheet.

multiple document interface: An interface that allows you to have several documents or document views open at the same time. Also called *multiple design interface*.

N

natural end: A type of coil end that occurs as the natural result of the pitch, revolution, height, and profile of the coil.

network: Several ribs or webs created using the same direction and thickness.

neutral axis: The axis of a bend radius where neither stretching nor compressing occurs.

nominal size: The designated size of a commercial product.

nominal value: The value of a commercial product; intended to be the true drawn size without any specified limits.

O

oblique view: A 3D view in which the plane of projection is parallel to the front surface, and a receding angle is applied.

offset: Form objects parallel to the specified geometry at a specified distance apart. When referring to the

Thicken/Offset
tool, the process of offsetting a surface from a face or surface, similar to offsetting a work plane from a face. When referring to threads, the distance from the edge of the face to the beginning of threads.

open loop: A sketch that includes a gap(s) between objects.

open sketch profile: A sketch profile that does not form a closed loop.

ordinate dimensioning: A dimensioning method that provides coordinates from established datums that are usually located at the corner of the part or the axis of a feature. Also called *rectangular coordinate dimensioning without dimension lines* or *arrowless dimensioning*.

origin: The center point (0,0,0) of the model's XYZ coordinate system.

orphaned annotations: Annotations that have been moved away from a drawing view associated with model geometry.

orthographic view: A 2D view, or projection, in which the line of sight is perpendicular to a surface, such as the front of an object or the XY plane.

over-constrained model: A model with too many constraints.

P

pan: Reposition the display of objects in the graphics window.

panel bar: A panel-like window that appears by default on the left side of the Inventor graphics window. Panel bars are the primary default location for accessing design tools.

parallel: A geometric construction that specifies that objects such as lines and ellipse axes will never intersect, no matter how long they become.

parameters: Characteristics that control the size, shape, and position of model geometry. Shape and size limits placed on sketches and features.

parametric solid modeling: A form of modeling in which parameters and constraints drive the model form and function to produce models that contain object volume and mass data that can be used to analyze internal and external object characteristics.

parent node: An item in the tree structure, similar to a folder, that is associated with subordinate child nodes.

part: An item or product or an element of an assembly.

partial auxiliary view: An auxiliary view that shows the true size and shape of only the inclined surface, eliminating any projected geometry that may be foreshortened.

parts list: A table that records and displays the parts and subassemblies used to create an assembly.

path: A guide, or route, for creating sketched features.

pattern occurrences: Representations of patterned features that identify how many features are present because of the pattern operation.

perpendicular: A geometric construction that defines a 90° angle between objects such as lines and ellipse axes.

pitch: The distance parallel to the axis between a point on one coil spiral to the corresponding point on the next coil spiral. (Ch. 5) The distance parallel to the axis from a point on one thread to the corresponding point on the next thread.

pivot point: The point that acts as the center point when you are viewing and rotating model space objects.

placed features: Features added to an existing feature without using a sketch.
placed sections: Loft sections that are created without a sketch and are placed along a selected centerline. Placed sections are calculated based on the loft cross section at the selected location.

profile: The side or section outline of a sketched feature.

projects: Files that manage and organize folders and files for specific design jobs.

promote: Add to the part environment. Remove parts from a subassembly and make them individual parts in the parent assembly.

pull direction: The direction in which the casting mold is pulled or removed from the part.

pull-down menus: A text-based menu input system in which menu items appear when you pick the menu name.

punch: A press or similar tool used to form a specific shape or hole in sheet metal. Also called a *sheet metal punch*.

Q

quilt: A set of combined surfaces.

R

radius: The distance from the center of a circle or arc to its circumference.

radius dimension: A dimension used to define the radius of an arc or circular feature.

rail: A 2D or 3D sketched curve that is used in conjunction with sections to manipulate and further control the loft shape.

read-only: A file open option that allows you to view a file, but not make changes to it.

realtime zooming: Zooming that can be viewed as it is performed.

rectangular coordinate dimensioning without dimension lines: A dimensioning method that provides coordinates from established datums that are usually located at the corner of the part or the axis of a feature. Also called *ordinate dimensioning* or *arrowless dimensioning*.

rectangular feature pattern: Occurrences of features copied and positioned a specified distance apart, in rows and columns.

rectangular pattern: An arrangement of copies of a feature into a designated number of rows and columns placed a specified distance apart.

regular polygon: A geometric shape with three or more sides, such as a triangle, square, or hexagon, with all sides being equal in length and symmetrical about a common center.

revision table: A table that records drawing changes; usually placed in the upper-right corner of the drawing. Also called a *revision* *history block* or *revision block*.

revision tag: A symbol that identifies the location at which the engineering change occurs. The tag corresponds to a specific entry in the revision table. Also called a *revision symbol*.

revolution: A feature created in a circular path around an axis; also called a *revolved feature*. In a coil, one complete spiral, or 360° loop.

revolved feature: A feature created in a circular path around an axis. Also known as a *revolution*.

rib: A closed section of material usually added to reinforce a part without adding excessive material or weight.

right-hand threads: Threads that move a right-hand threaded bolt forward in a clockwise direction

rounds: Rounded exterior corners; rounds remove material from corners. A curve placed on the exterior intersection of two or more faces, removing material from a feature.

S

scale factor: The amount of enlargement or reduction.

screen space: A space, or environment, in which the graphics window controls model display; the center is located at the center of the graphics window.

sculpt: The process of using intersecting surfaces to add or remove solid mass.

sections: Sketches and existing feature faces used to develop loft features. A view that splits a part along a cutting-plane line to expose the interior features of the part. Also called a *section view*.

section view: A view that splits a part along a cutting-plane line to expose the interior features of the part. Also called a *section*.

setback: Point at which a fillet or round on one edge begins to combine with a fillet or round of at least two other edges.

shared content: Files available on the Internet, such as bolts from a bolt manufacturer, or components accessible on an intranet system, such as standard parts that are used for developing assemblies. Also called *third-party content*.

sharing: Making a sketch available for additional features after it has been used to create a feature.

sheet formats: Predefined, multiview drawing sheet templates that contain a default border and title block for various standard sheet sizes.

sheet metal punch: A press or similar tool used to form a specific shape or hole in sheet metal. Also called a *punch*.

shell: An operation that removes material from a feature and creates a hollow space or opening.

shortcut keys: Keyboard key combinations that allow you to access predefined tools.

shortcut menus: Menus that allow access to tools and options by right-clicking anywhere in the graphics window or on an object or selection.

sketch: A 2D drawing that provides the profile and/or guide for developing a sketched feature.

sketch center points: Points used to define the location of center points for features that reference center points, such as holes and sheet metal punches.

sketched features: Features such as extrusions, revolutions, sweeps, lofts, and coils that are built from a sketch.

sketch helix: A winding spiral shape primarily used to create springs, detailed threads, and similar items.

sketch pattern: Multiple arranged copies, or a pattern, of sketch shapes.

sketch points: Points used for construction purposes to help you develop sketch geometry.

spacing: In patterning, the distance between occurrences based on the width of the selected features and the distance between the copies.

specific notes: Notes that apply to a specific feature or features on the drawing. Also called *local notes*.

spline: A complex curve defined by control points along the curve.

split: A feature that removes a portion of a model or divides faces at a separation sketch or plane.

spotface: Similar to a counterbore, but shallower; typically applied when a flush surface is necessary, such as to hide a flat washer, or in casting applications.

standard: A set of styles and other general drawing preferences that has been agreed upon and recommended for use by an industry, government, military, or standardssetting organization.

steering wheels: Circular navigation tools that allow you to navigate around a model.

stitched: Two or more surfaces combined to form a single surface or quilt. supplement)

style library: A folder, Design Data by default, that houses styles in XML file format.

subassembly: An assembly placed in a larger assembly, such as switch, or spring assembly; subassemblies may be used more than once in the final assembled product.

surface extrusion: A volume less shape that is primarily used for construction purposes, allowing you to generate advanced models.

surface finish: The allowable roughness, waviness, lay, and flaws on a surface.

sweep: A feature created by guiding, or sweeping, a sketch profile along a sketch path.

T

table-driven iFeature: An iFeature that allows you to create multiple variations of the original iFeature using information stored in a spreadsheet.

tabular dimensioning: A type of arrowless dimensioning in which coordinate dimensions and size dimensions are given in a table that correlates with features on the drawing with a hole tag.

tangent constraint: A geometric construction that specifies how a curve touches another curve at the point of tangency.

tap: Use a machine tool to form an interior thread.

tapered threads: Threads often used for pipe fittings when a liquid or airtight seal is required.

templates: Files with predefined settings used to begin new documents.

thickening: The process of adding a solid to a face or surface, similar to a solid extrusion.

third-party content: Files available on the Internet, such as bolts from a bolt manufacturer, or components accessible on an intranet system, such as standard parts that are used for developing assemblies. Also called *shared content*.

thread class: The designated amount, or grade, of tolerance specified for the thread, ranging from fine to coarse threads.

threads: Grooves cut in a spiral fashion in or around the face of a cylindrical or conical feature.

title block: An area on the drawing sheet that contains information about the model, company, drafter, tolerances, and other design information.

tolerance stack: Text that is stacked horizontally without a fraction bar.

tool buttons: Buttons in a toolbar, each with a specific icon, that activate a tool or option.

tooltip: A small text box that displays when you hover over a button, giving information about the function of the button.

trails: Connection graphics between components that show their relative positions in the assembly.

transitional constraints: Constraints that identify relationships between the transitioning path of a fixed component and a component moving along the path.

transition angle: The number of degrees a coil end travels, or transitions, with pitch.

tweaks: Component modifications made during the preparation of a presentation.

U

under-constrained model: A model with elements that are unclear, can be changed or moved, or remain undefined.

user interface: The tools and techniques used to provide information to and receive information from a computer application. Also called an *interface*.

user parameters: Additional parameters defined by the user.

V

variable fillets and rounds: Fillets and rounds that have different curved radii placed at precise points between the start and end of a feature edge.

vertex: When referring to filet and round setbacks, the intersection of three or more edges.

virtual component: An assembly component used primarily to define a separate bill of materials item, without creating a model.

void: Any set of internal feature faces that define a hollow area in a solid.

W

walk-through: A viewing process that shows how it would look if you could walk in and around the actual product you are modeling.

web: An open section of material usually added to reinforce a part without adding excessive material or weight.

wedges: The parts of a steering wheel that contain navigation tools.

weldment: An assembly in which parts are fixed together with welds.

wireframe model: A model that contains only information about model edges and the intersection of edges.

wireframe representation: A display in which surfaces are removed so that you can see the edges clearly.

work axis: An axis used to create construction lines and axes. A parametric reference line that can be located anywhere in space.

work features: Features that direct the location and arrangement of other features. Construction points, lines, and surfaces that create reference elements anywhere in space to help position and generate additional features.

work planes: Planes that are used to create construction planes. Flat reference surfaces that can be located anywhere in space.

work points: Points used to create construction points. Parametric reference points that can be located on any part feature or in 3D space.

workspace: The default folder where files are located in a project.

Z

zoom in: Increase the displayed size of objects in the graphics window to view a smaller portion of the model, but in greater detail.

zoom out: Reduce the displayed size of objects in the graphics window to display more of the model, but in view less detail.

www.ingramcontent.com/pod-product-compliance
Lightning Source LLC
Chambersburg PA
CBHW082208300426
44117CB00016B/2720